Chartres Labyrinth
Construction Manual

by

Robert D. Ferré

Revised April, 2003
Reprinted May, 2006
Expanded Veriditas Digital Version, 2014

ISBN: 978-1-940875-90-3

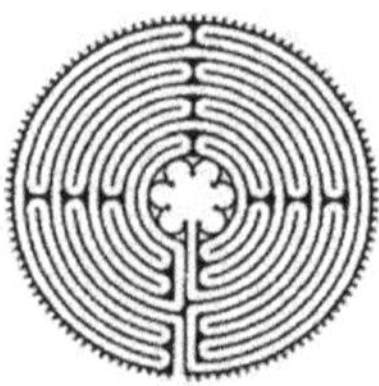

Published by Labyrinth Enterprises, LLC
www.labyrinth-enterprises.com
(800) 873-9873

The Labyrinth Series

Five books written by Robert D. Ferré are part of the Labyrinth Series published by Labyrinth Enterprises, LLC, and currently being reissued in a digital format for the special Veriditas Edition. After these are all issued, more titles will follow.

The Labyrinth Revival: A Personal Account from the Front Lines

First Edition: 1997
Second Edition: 2002
Expanded Veriditas Digital Edition: Planned for 2015

Church Labyrinths: Questions & answers regarding the history, relevance, and use of labyrinths in churches

First Edition: 2001
Digital Edition: 2013
Expanded Veriditas Digial Edition: Planned for 2015

Origin, Symbolism, and Design of the Chartres Labyrinth

First Edition: 2001
Expanded Veriditas Digital Edition: Planned for 2015

Chartres Labyrinth: Construction Manual

First edition: 2001
Revised edition: 2003
Expanded Veriditas Digital Edition: 2014

Classical Labyrinths: Construction Manual

First Edition: 2002
Veriditas Digital Edition: Planned for 2015

New:

Canvas Labyrinths: Construction Manual

Veriditas Digital Edition: July, 2014

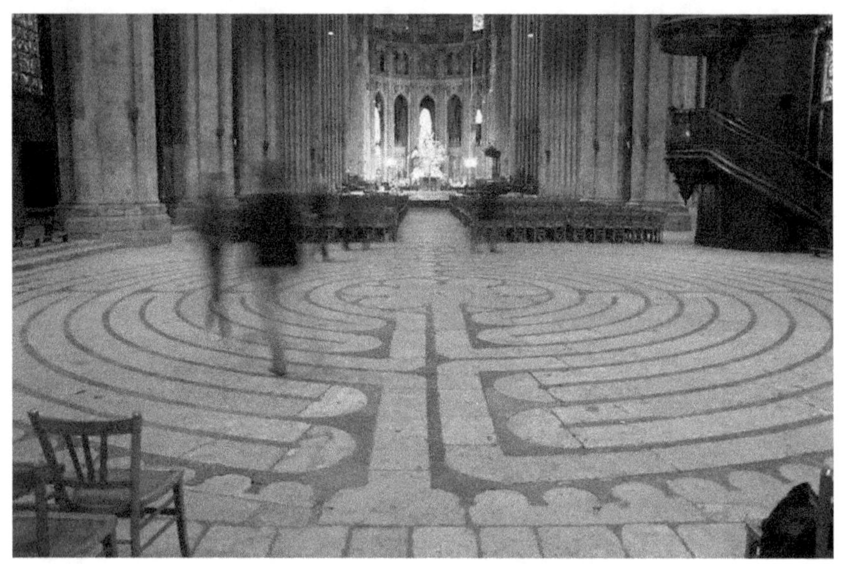

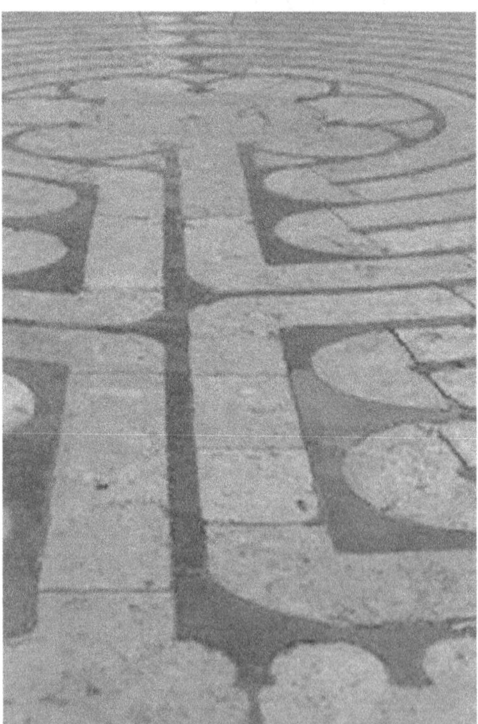

A marvelous site for images of Chartres Cathedral is:

http://images.library.pitt.edu/c/chartres/

These photos were taken by Philip Maye.

For being more than 800 years old, the labyrinth is in reasonably good shape.

TABLE OF CONTENTS

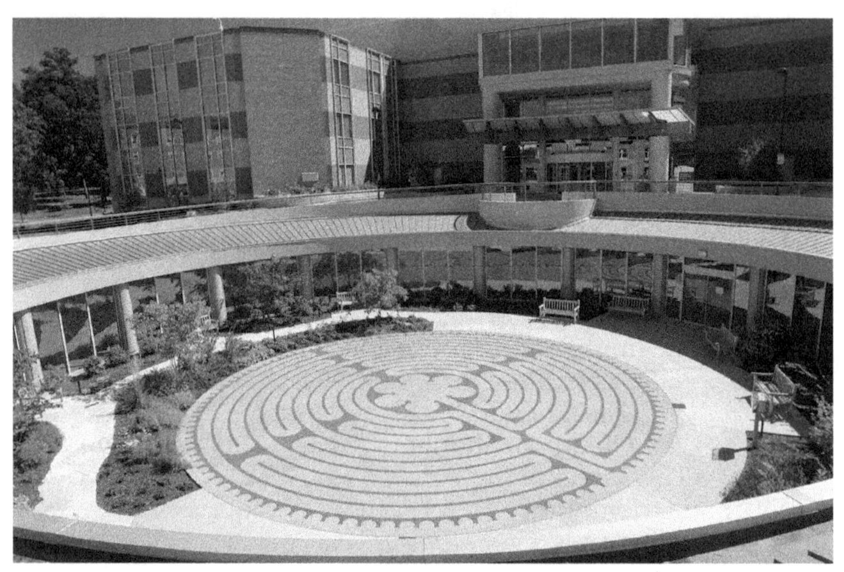

Chartres labyrinth at Marianjoy Rehabilitation Hospital in Wheaton, Illinois

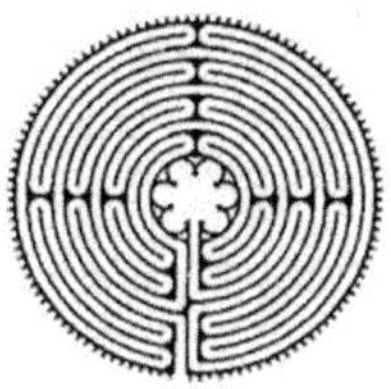

New Veriditas Digital Edition

I made my first canvas labyrinth in 1995 at the urging of the Rev. Dr. Lauren Artress, who had just founded Veriditas, a nonprofit organization to train facilitators and promote the effective use of labyrinths. That request led to my becoming a full time labyrinth maker, with Veriditas as my first client.

Both Veriditas and my company, Labyrinth Enterprises, LLC (originally the St. Louis Labyrinth Project), have been through many changes over the years. We've had good times and lean times. We've traveled together in France and Germany, visiting Chartres Cathedral and Hildegard of Bingen sites. Through it all, my assistants and I supplied Veriditas with canvas labyrinths, hundreds of them.

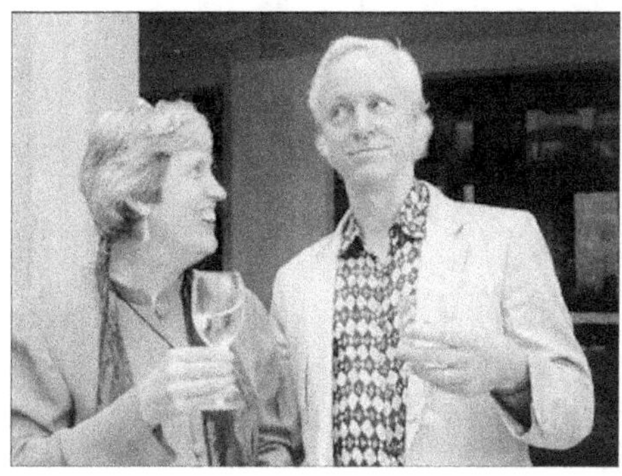

Lauren and Robert: A light moment together at Maison St. Yves. in Chartres.

Now, I'm mostly retired, and Lauren is heading in the same direction. Capable hands have honed Veriditas into an effective organization with deeply meaningful events. A number of master teachers are adding to the thousands of facilitators already trained.

I'm passing my duties as a labyrinth maker to colleagues whom I've helped train and who will likewise continue carrying the torch for the next generation.

The proceeds from my labyrinth books, updated and reissued in special digital editions, go to Veriditas. I can think of no better tribute to honor the two decades we have worked together.

It's a simple matter to make changes to the text. I welcome your comments, corrections, and suggestions. You can reach me at:

robert@labyrinth-enterprises.com

Many thanks.

Robert D. Ferré
September, 2014

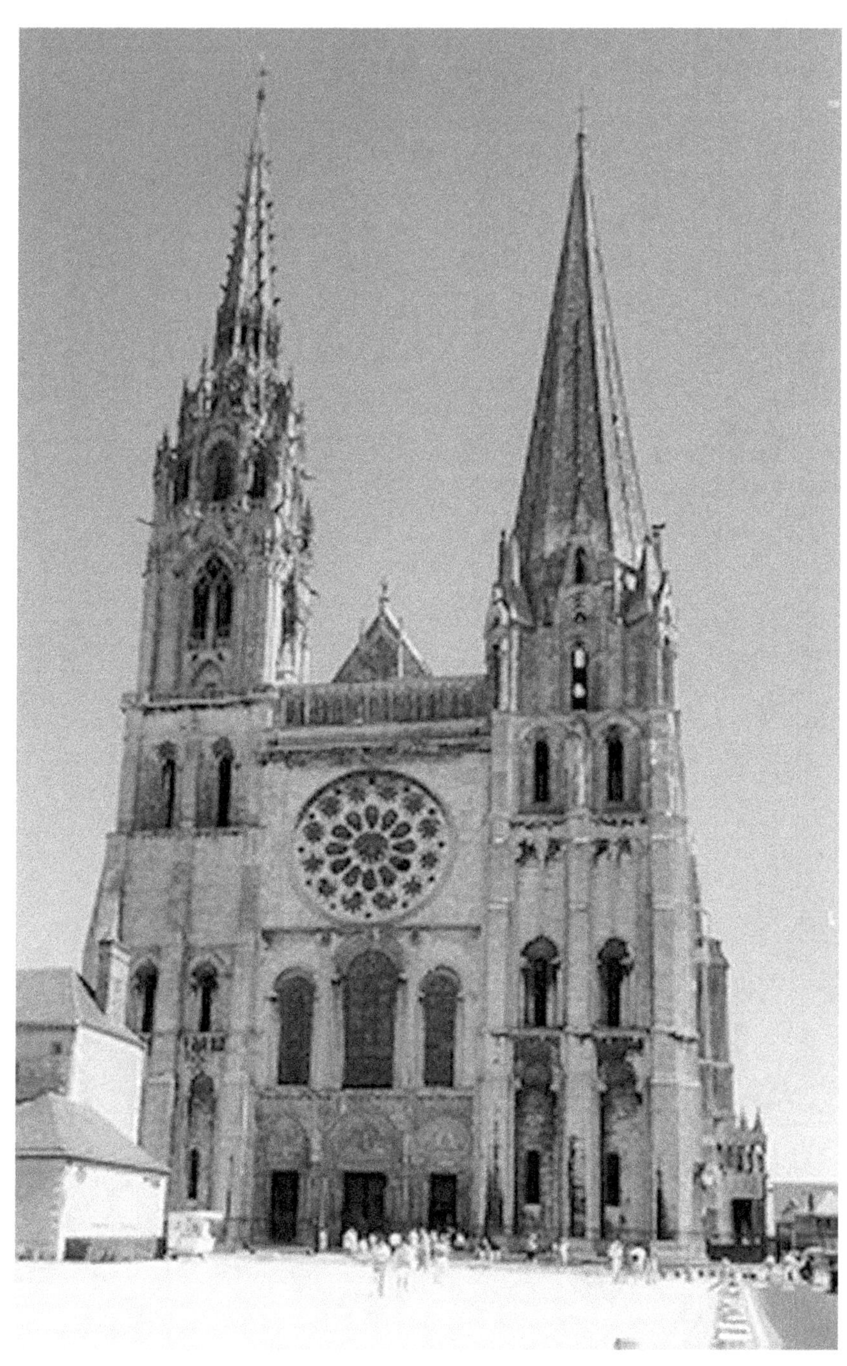

Chartres Cathedral with its distinctive dissimilar towers

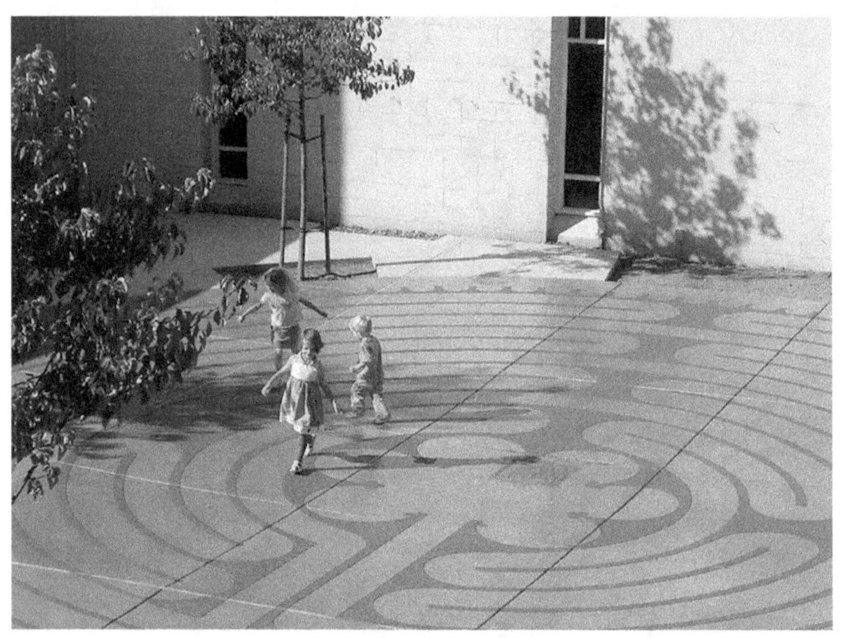

Chartres labyrinth at First Presbyterian Church in Livermore, California

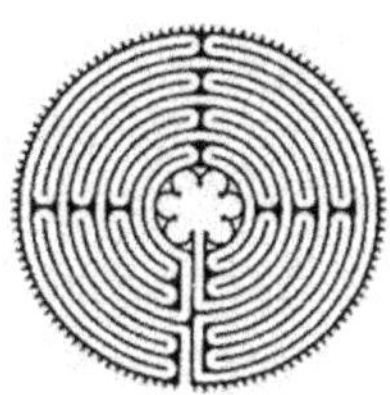

History

Eight hundred and twenty years ago, the greatest mason of his era was called to Chartres to lay out a new cathedral amidst the still-smoldering ashes of the old one. We don't know his name, so let's use the one assigned to him by John James: Scarlet. Part of the growing middle class, Scarlet would have been well-educated and affluent, part of the non-royal aristocracy.

He was likely an older man who had spent the previous thirty years working on churches, abbeys and cathedrals in the Paris Basin. Having assiduously kept abreast of new developments, about which word traveled rapidly through the mason's camps, he incorporated leading-edge technologies and features which had developed over the previous century's unprecedented building boom.

An architectural revolution was in progress, during which, for the first time in all of history, builders would overcome the limitations of stone. Greeks, Romans, Mayans, Egyptians—no previous culture had discovered the secret. Finally, in the twelfth century of the Christian era, ogival arches and flying buttresses made it possible for buildings to be tall and open, the walls thin, filled with huge windows. It was miraculous.

I remember standing with John James amidst the ruins of Longpont Abbey, examining what was certainly the work of Scarlet, finished ten years before he went to Chartres. The column pedestals were exactly the same. Nearby, in Braine, he had seen a new treatment for the triforium, which he was to use in Chartres.

I would love to tell the whole story here, but that will be the topic of a future book. Let me just use the metaphor of a symphony. Each new architectural discovery was like inventing an instrument. Finally, in Chartres, for the first time, the full symphony played. Scarlet was the conductor, and to some extent, the composer. Yes, others had invented most of the instruments, but Scarlet was the one who had the imagination and audacity to use them, to see their potential, to make them play beautiful music together.

It was a period Will Durant calls the Age of Faith, a time of peace, political stability, growing population, economic prosperity, dominance of the church, intellectual inquiry, and technological advance. Previously, the largest churches were abbeys, built in the countryside and inhabited by monks. Scarlet, in contrast, was building a cathedral in the city, for the secular clergy, the burgeoning urban population and the flourishing middle class.

Chartres Cathedral is the most admired, most written about, most influential structure in all of Europe, then and now. Philip Ball writes:

> *"There are few buildings in the world that exude such a sense of meaning, intention, signification . . . that tell you so clearly and so forcefully that these stones were put in place according to a philosophy of awesome proportions."*

The Romanesque church was itself a marvel, begun by Bishop Fulbert shortly after the year 1000, damaged by fire and then

Only one drawing exists of the Romanesque church, from which a more precise illustration was extrapolated (below).

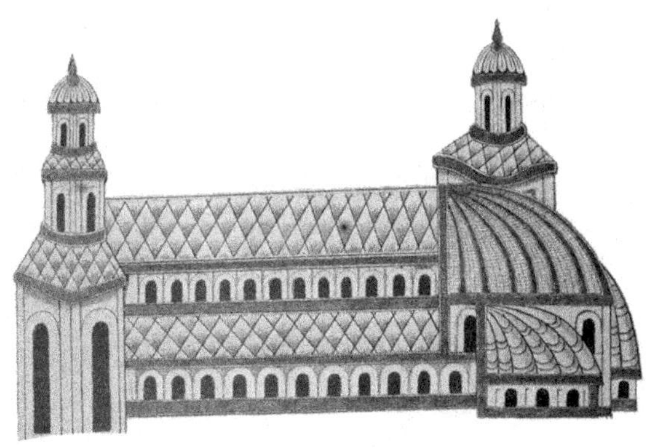

VUE DE LA CATHÉDRALE DE FULBERT, D'APRÈS ANDRÉ DE MICI

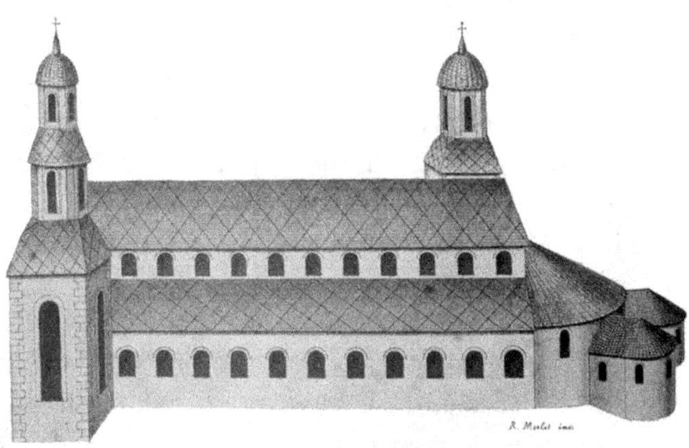

VUE PERSPECTIVE DE LA CATHÉDRALE DE FULBERT RESTITUÉE

enlarged a century later with the addition of two towers and a narthex. It had the largest crypt in France, built to accommodate the flood of pilgrims who came to pay homage to the Virgin Mary at this, her favorite church. On at least four other occasions churches on this site had burned, and most of the town with them. Now it had happened again, on June 10, 1194. The Virgin's veil, the sacred relic given to the cathedral in 876 by Charles the Bald, grandson of Charlemagne, was saved. The town and the clergy were determined to rebuild.

And so they called in Scarlet. He must have taken quite a while to determine the complete plan. The windows and iconography express the theological story they wanted to tell. The entire cathedral, in all of its many aspects, has a single, unified purpose: To symbolize our journey from this world to the next, from earth to heaven, from sin to salvation.

Perhaps it was Scarlet who suggested the labyrinth. The basic path pattern had already been devised over several centuries of manuscript drawings. Scarlet (or the clergy who advised him) added the proportions, the petals, and the lunations, all reflecting the dedication of the cathedral to the Virgin Mary. (See *Origin, Symbolism, and Design of the Chartres Labyrinth.*)

Scarlet laid out the plan for the cathedral. Later, in 1201, he built the labyrinth. In 1215, he returned again to build the great western window. Perhaps the labyrinth was Scarlet's signature. There's historical evidence to suggest that medieval masons held in high regard the mythical first architect and craftsman, Daedalus, who built the labyrinth (maze) that imprisoned the Minotaur.

To assure that people would make the connection, the center of the labyrinth originally had a plaque portraying Theseus in combat with the Minotaur. I have read speculations that the center may have contained something else, such as images of the architects, as in Amiens.

Such was not the case. According to an account by the mayor of Chartres of the removal of the central plaque during the Napoleonic War, the original image was very worn and hard to see, apparently an engraving rather than bas relief.

Many like to say that Theseus represents Christ, overcoming sin (Minotaur). But Christ wouldn't have needed Ariadne's thread. So I think Theseus is each of us, on his or her spiritual quest, overcoming our difficulties and darkest tendencies. In

Christian terms, Ariadne symbolizes Mary, who provided the thread (the teachings of the church, through Jesus) to give us guidance.

What's the meaning of the labyrinth? It's about our spiritual journey. The stories told in the windows, the statuary, the liturgy, the architecture, the sacred geometry — everything informs the process of salvation. Surely it's no different for the labyrinth.

That there's only one path, with nothing up to the walker to decide, may have been a deliberate statement by the church that it had a monopoly on heaven. We can only surmise such meaning, however, as no one bothered to write it down. Perhaps some medieval volume in the archives in Chartres contained an important passage, but that building was burned to the ground by American bombing in World War II.

Many books and websites declare that the labyrinth served as a substitute form of pilgrimage when it was too dangerous to make a journey to the Holy Land. Some even suggest that going to Jerusalem once in their lifetime was a requirement of all Christians. Clearly they are confusing the Hajj, and pilgrimage to Mecca by Muslims. There was no such requirement for Christians.

Description historique et statistique de la ville de Reims, by E. B. F. Gérusez, published in 1817, stands as the first known reference to using the labyrinth as a form of pilgrimage, either as a substitute or for its own merits. Perhaps he was speculating about the labyrinth in the cathedral in Reims, which had been removed almost forty years earlier (1778).

In reality, only a century after the labyrinth was built, people were already pondering its meaning and purpose. No contemporary source exists to give us a clue. In the fourteenth century a rule was passed forbidding people from dancing on the labyrinth. Hm-m-m-m-m-m.

Laid across the entire nave from pillar to pillar, the labyrinth was meticulously carved out of four-inch-thick limestone from the nearby quarries in Berchères-les-Pierres. The rest of the floor and most of the cathedral (not to mention half the town buildings, the curbs, some benches) are built from the same excellent stone which, although porous and filled with tiny holes, gets harder with age and more durable. The lines for the labyrinth pattern were constructed from a blue/black marble probably mined in the Picardy area, north of Paris.

Were there any earlier walkable labyrinths, built before the Chartres labyrinth? It's hard to tell. Chartres was part of the diocese of Sens, a city 170 kilometers to the east, and we know Sens had a labyrinth. It could have been roughly contemporary. Craig Wright and others have found three different designs that have been attributed to the Sens labyrinth, all of which had a common feature: They only had concentric circles. Chartres is unique in having the six petals in the center and the lunations (arcs) around the perimeter.

Early scholars, such as W. H. Matthews (*Mazes and Labyrinths*, 1922) describe several labyrinths in Italy that apparently predate Chartres. Their small size (five to eleven feet in diameter) raises the question of whether they were symbolic decoration, based on manuscript drawings, or were intended to be walked.

Matthews quotes several interesting passages. One, by P. M. Campi (1651), locates the labyrinth in juxtaposition to the signs of the zodiac. At the time Chartres Cathedral was built, clocks had not yet been invented. (The large clock on the north side of the building was added in the fifteenth century.) Calendars were the reference to passing time, as portrayed by the signs of the zodiac, commonly paired with the labor of that season (harvesting, etc.).

In other words, time is passing, we'd better get on with seeking our salvation. Campi also included a quatrain to the effect that when we get caught up in the wiles of the world, we can regain the correct doctrine (path) only with difficulty. Similarly, a Latin phrase accompanying the finger labyrinth on the wall of the cathedral of San Martino in Lucca, states that Daedalus built it and no one can escape without the help of Ariadne (reinterpreted in context as the Virgin Mary).

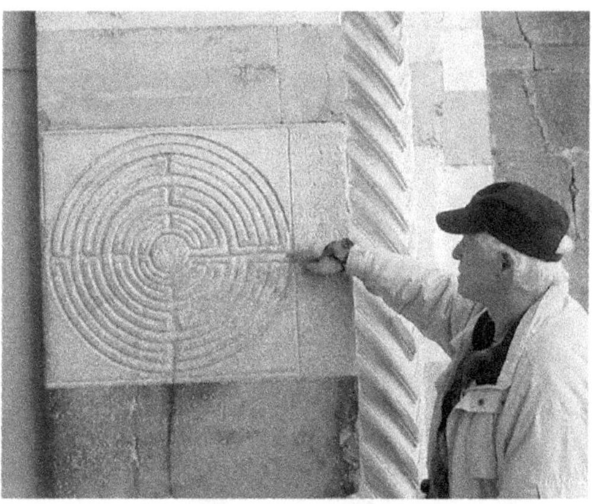

Me in Lucca. Note that the entrance to the labyrinth is on the right side. The Latin inscription is to the right, partly hidden by the pillar.

Besides the sheer difficulty of our journey through life, Matthews repeats from a J. Durand (no date) the idea that the Italian labyrinths pertained to the various degrees of beatitude by which the soul approaches heaven, as figured by Dante (a popular association between Dante and labyrinths). Again, this would be consistent with the theme of Chartres Cathedral as described above.

Dating labyrinths is an inexact science. The one in Ravenna was once thought to date from the seventh century, but now is considered to date to 1540. Missing the date by nine hundred years is rather significant. Matthews suggests that the San Savino labyrinth was formally consecrated on 15 August 1107. So, clearly, some of the Italian designs, whether walked or not, predated Chartres.

We might say the symbol was in vogue in the Middle Ages. Yet, in my mind, as he did with so many other elements, Scarlet took the concept to new heights, making the largest of any church floor labyrinth with little doubt it was meant to be walked. I think his inspiration came not from Italy but from manuscripts, as previously stated, many of which were produced in the Cistercian Monastery in Pontigy, near Auxerre close by.

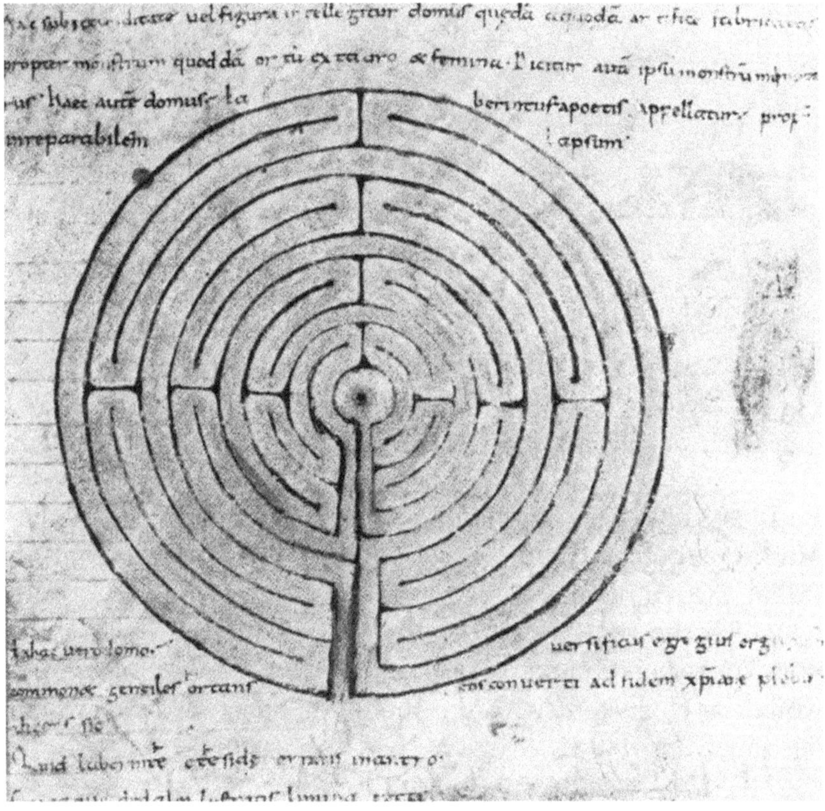

Experimental drawings in manuscripts slowly developed the medieval pattern. This one, dating from the tenth century, clearly shows the ultimate path pattern used at Chartres.

Chartres Cathedral was constructed at a time when great devotion was informed by arduous intellectual rigor, a combination of both faith and reason. Even as it was being built, secular universities were being founded. The world changed quickly, aided by the inquisition, the Black Plague, the

Hundred Years War, the Reformation and subsequent religious wars, the Renaissance and the Age of Enlightenment.

Chartres was the apogee of a theology and worldview that was soon lost. Very quickly not only the labyrinth but the whole cathedral became anachronistic. It represented a different age and mindset. Its meaning was forgotten, its purpose ignored, its beauty overlooked.

Fortunately for us, plans to destroy the cathedral (an ignominious fate suffered by many great abbey churches) were foiled and it survived to the modern era, where it has undergone a rebirth of global scope (see *The Labyrinth Revival*).

Did Scarlet make more than one labyrinth? We have no way of knowing. Little would he have suspected that in the twenty-first century thousands of examples of his design (plus many variations) would be constructed.

This brief history gives an insight into the origins of the Chartres labyrinth. I have measured it many times, which leads me to one last story. The stone around the perimeter of the labyrinth is very irregular. Given the precision of the rest of the construction, this must have been deliberate. Perhaps it was intended to make a distinct demarkation from the rest of the floor.

Whatever the case, the lunations were carved in different quantities. Some stones have a single lunation, whereas others have two or three. In six cases there are four lunations carved into one stone. Five of these are identical, with a variation of only one-sixteenth of an inch over an expanse of more than four feet. That's an amazing degree of accuracy. The final one, however, is two inches bigger! I think they got to the end of the lunations and found they had a little extra space, causing them to fudge a bit. Those particular lunations are almost half an inch larger than all the others. (I'll be repeating this story again when we learn about the lunations.)

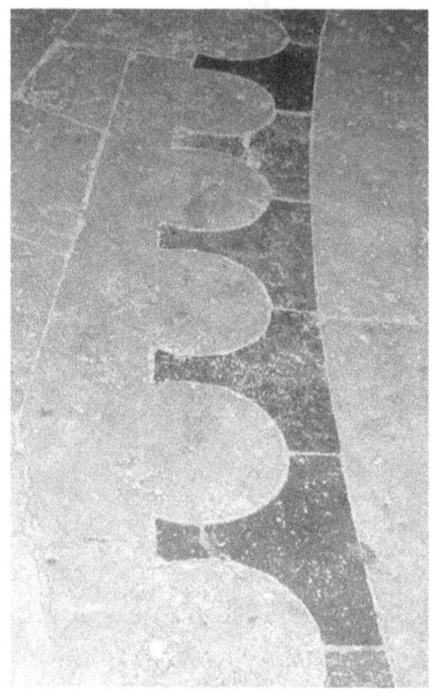

Lunations. Can you spot the nineteenth century repair? Note that four complete lunation circles (not the black teeth) are cut into one stone. This is the one larger than the others.

Skilled craftsmanship isn't always about being perfect. In some cases necessity requires creative adjustments and solutions. Chartres Cathedral is filled with obvious discrepancies and irregularities, yet everything has been assembled with exquisite adroitness.

In my trainings I encourage people to make labyrinths even if they are less than perfect. I know of several very crude and inaccurate approximations of the Chartres labyrinth which have been used very lovingly and effectively. Don't hesitate to make your own labyrinth because you don't think it will be good enough. Do your part, to the best of your ability, and the labyrinth itself will take care of the rest. Disarm your inner critic and press ahead, even if the final product is less than perfect.

Having said that, I am not giving you permission to be sloppy, lazy, rushed, or impatient. Aspiring to make a credible copy is a worthy endeavor. Use the labyrinth to focus your energy and accomplish your finest work, in the service of others, requesting and receiving divine assistance all the way.

Chartres cathedral is a great example of such devoted craftsmanship. High up at the roof level on the south choir is a stone of unbelievable size and complexity. There is a built-in railing for the adjacent walkway, a change of direction, a slot to allow light into a little storeroom, plus tenons that would have gone out into mortises of adjacent stones. The whole stone must weigh two or three tons. It had to be lifted by man-powered cranes and moved into place.

That stone is truly magnificent, and also puzzling. Why not just use many small stones? It would have been much easier. This extraordinary example of some stone cutter's skill is high up and out of view from almost everyone except those on the upper walkway. The workers were constructing God's home on earth, and an homage to the Virgin whom they adored. It was not a question of doing things the easy way. Just the opposite. They wanted their work to represent their skill and their faith. That huge stone ties that wall together in a way smaller stones would not.

We must assign Scarlet a name because he left no trace of his carved anywhere. That great mason remains anonymous. His creation was not about seeking personal recognition. Later in the Renaissance, art would become secular, and artists would become stars, proudly signing their own work. But not Scarlet.

For that reason, I never sign any of my work. It doesn't seem fitting for me to take credit in the face of such humility.

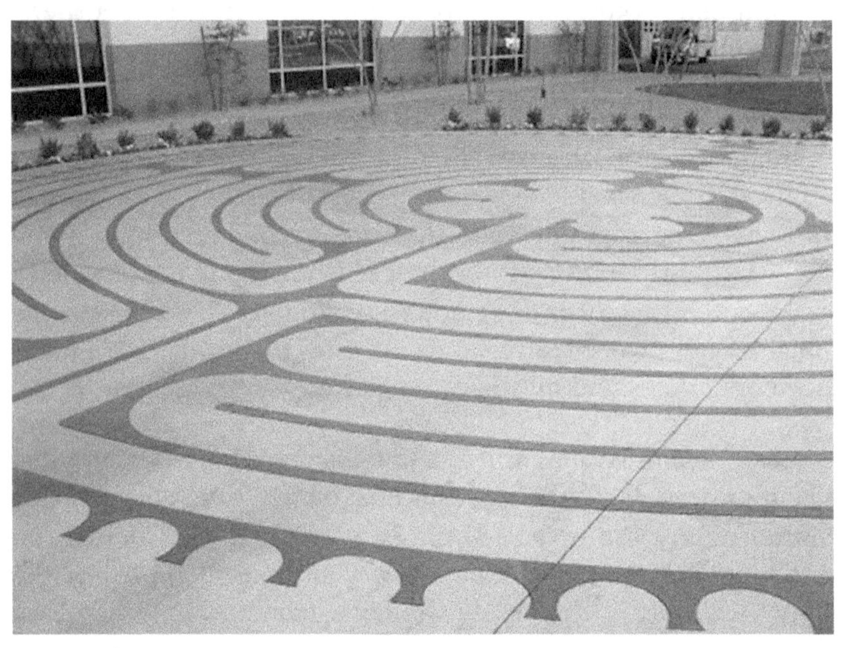

Chartres labyrinth at Dominican Rose Hospital in Las Vegas, Nevada (Saint Martin Campus)

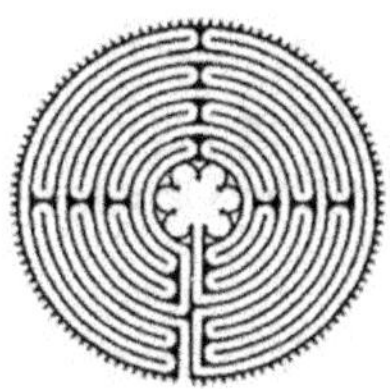

Measurements and Proportions

Through the years, the measurements of the Chartres labyrinth have remained elusive. Several writers in the nineteenth and early twentieth centuries published very disparate figures, sometimes varying by several inches. Marcel Bulteau said it was 12.5 meters, Edmont Suyez found 12.3 meters, Emanuel Waller gave 13 meters, while Maurice Guinguand found it 12. 3 meters (north-south) by 12.6 meters (east-west). The difference between 12.3 and 13 meters is more than 27 inches!

By the way, it isn't elliptical. Perhaps the writer was looking at a famous photograph, taken from the keyhole of the vault, which isn't directly above the center of the labyrinth. The slight angle gives it an elliptical shape. One writer said the lines were made of lead, and another the labyrinth was made of blue and white tiles. Did they ever even see the labyrinth?

Can't we just stretch a tape measure across the floor and read off the numbers? It's not that easy. I have measured it in detail numerous times, as well as making some direct floor rubbings, constantly revising my numbers.

The labyrinth is in remarkably good condition, considering it's more than eight centuries old. Labyrinths in some of the other cathedrals were lost because the floor wore out and needed to be redone. It was too costly to replace the labyrinth. Besides, it was during a period when labyrinths were out of favor.

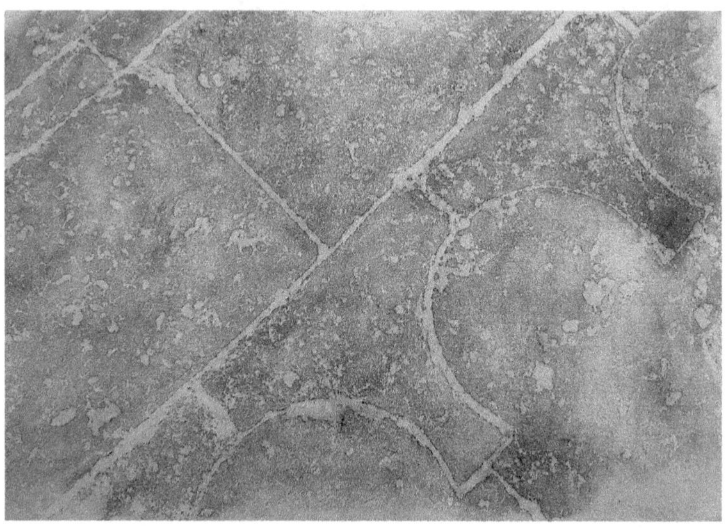

One of my floor rubbings. Note the difference in the mortar width in the one complete lunation circle, left side and right side. The stone is very porous, as shown by the light areas.

Then there's the matter of the mortar. The labyrinth is made of beige limestone and blue-black marble. The line is the black color, then a path of beige, then a black line, etc. However, in between these, is mortar, which can vary from one-fourth inch to three-fourths inch in width.

Now, when we make a canvas labyrinth, or a concrete labyrinth, or even one made of pavers, there's no intervening mortar space. An exception is the indoor stone labyrinth at Grace Cathedral, which was laid like tile with a grout space between the pieces, thus approximating the original.

So, what does one do with the mortar—incorporate it into the line or the path? Or split the difference? Each alternative produces a different set of numbers and proportions.

Due to the age of the labyrinth, the edges of the stone are worn and ragged. Measuring the labyrinth requires taking an average of several measurements of the same element (line, path, etc.). The petal crosses, for example, have reached such a state of irregularity that I have come up with two or three possible geometric solutions.

I'm not the only person to face this task. Australian architect John James studied Chartres Cathedral stone by stone over a period of five years, taking thousands of measurements. To measure the labyrinth, he used several wires that were pulled tight to avoid any looseness or sagging.

In comparing my measurements with his (I just used a tape measure), I find that we closely agree. In 2012, I spent a day with John James at his 240-acre retreat in the Blue Mountains, west of Syndey, Australia. Together we compared notes. I pointed out some inconsistencies in his two-volume description of Chartres Cathedral (*The Contractors of Chartres*) and he considered the proportions I use. Our measurements were in metric scale, which is a lot easier to divide into small units, unlike Imperial feet and inches.

A clue to the measurements and proportions can also be found in the foot measure used by Scarlet. He used two, the Roman Foot (295 mm) and the *pes manualis* (354 mm). By having two different scales, it's possible to incorporate more symbolic proportions.

Different masons used different foot measures. A common one was *pied-du-roi*, 325 mm. We give these values in metric scale now, but of course that didn't exist back then. In fact, when they built Chartres Cathedral, they were still using Roman numerals. Once Scarlet laid out the plan for the cathedral, however, subsequent masons would have been obliged to use his foot measure in most cases.

Despite our efforts that day in Australia, we could not get our measurements to come out exactly. We always had to make some small adjustments. It's as if the labyrinth refuses to be captured in such literal terms.

On yet another occasion, I went to Chartres with the architects planning the Cathedral Labyrinth in New Harmony, Indiana, a magnificent replica of the Chartres labyrinth. We spent hours taking measurements.

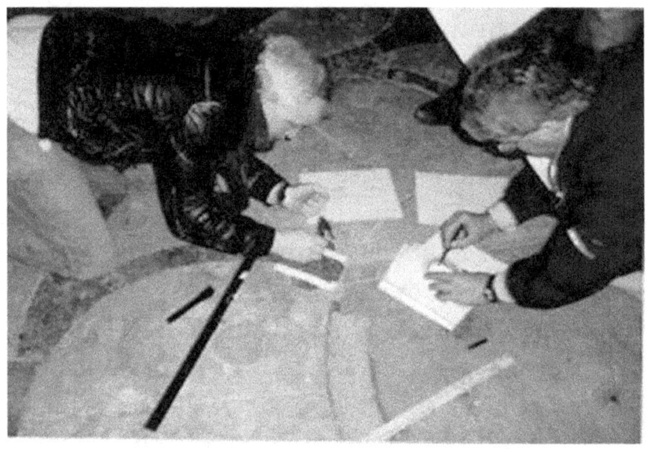

Here I am measuring the labyrinth in Chartres Cathedral with architect Rob Sovinski

I found that using one set of proportions worked for smaller areas, but when multiplied over the whole labyrinth did not come out exactly right. Having taken all of the above factors into consideration, I have come up with a set of measurements that I think most suits the intent of the builders and the intended symbolism. They involve slight compromises. To verify them, I have drawn the labyrinth on the computer in CAD, which does not fudge anything. In constructing polymer concrete labyrinths, we score the pattern into the concrete with diamond-bladed saws. Again, we have to use precise measurements.

Here are some links to further discussions about size:

http://www.labyrinthos.net/chartresfaq.html

http://blogmymaze.wordpress.com/2011/02/11/how-long-is-the-path-in-the-chartres-labyrinth/

http://www.labyrinth-enterprises.com/FAQ005.html

The Measurements

The Chartres labyrinth, including the lunations, measures 42' 3⅜" (' = feet," = inches, hence, forty-two feet, three and three-eighths inches). This is too large to reproduce in most indoor settings. I have never made a full size replica inside a church. Nor would the labyrinth fit into the nave of any other major Gothic church in France, even though some buildings are larger overall than Chartres.

It would take a gymnasium or ballroom to accommodate a canvas labyrinth of that size. So at Labyrinth Enterprises, our standard size for a canvas Chartres labyrinth was thirty-six feet in diameter for the canvas, and thus slightly under thirty-five feet for the pattern itself. We didn't arrive at that size by attempting a ⅚ reduction. The canvas that we used came in six foot widths, so our standard sizes were twenty-four, thirty, and thirty-six feet.

I believe that thirty feet is really the smallest usable size for the Chartres pattern (see photo next page). Nevertheless, I found on the Internet a group in England that has one that's five meters in diameter (a little over sixteen feet). It would be a challenge to walk paths that narrow.

Outdoors, of course, it's possible to make the labyrinth in full scale, or even more. The largest one I know of is 180 feet across, mowed into a meadow—far too long to walk easily.

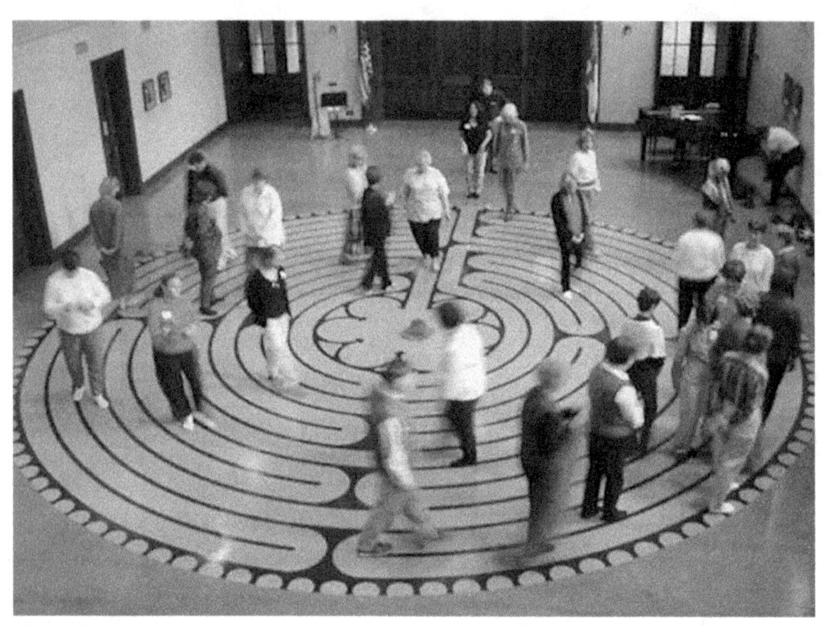

A thirty-foot diameter Chartres pattern, the smallest I would recommend.

At Unity Village in Lee Summit, Missouri, they thought they needed the paths wide enough to hold a wheel chair, so they ended up with a labyrinth more than 100 feet in diameter. Ironically, it's too long for anyone in a wheelchair to manage. Even able bodied walkers find that the length turns out to be an endurance test, losing all meditative value.

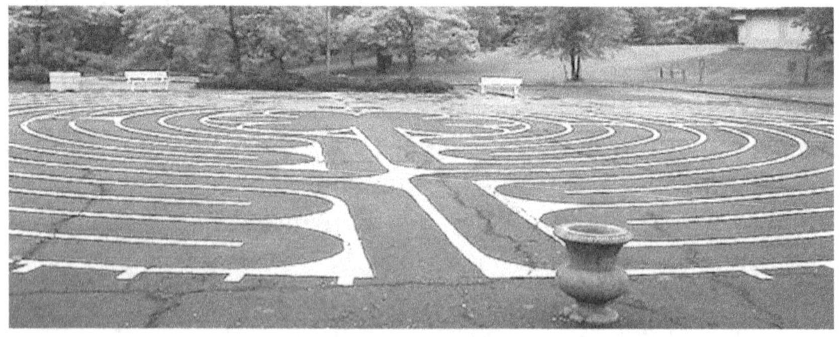

Unity Village labyrinth, more than 100 feet in diameter

At the Mercy Center in Saint Louis, Missouri, sixteen years ago, I helped to make a rock-and-mulch labyrinth that's eighty feet in diameter. The lines are white stones and the paths black rubber tire mulch. Given the plantings and the pleasant setting, the size doesn't seem overwhelming.

I was amused by the sapling they planted in the center, thinking that it would someday shade the labyrinth. But look at the following photo, taken ten years later.

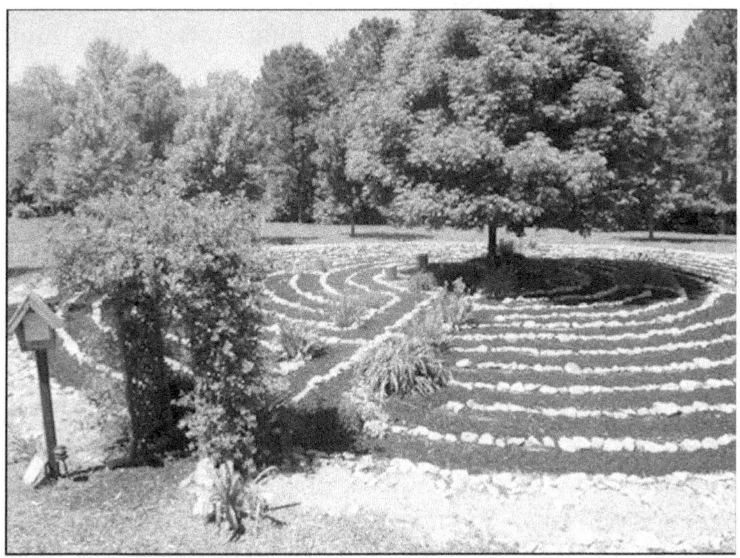

The St. Louis Mercy Center labyrinth at ten years old (now fifteen).

Now it's over fifteen years old and they have planted trees around the perimeter. It won't be long before the branches will meet and what was once an open field will be a lush, shaded labyrinth.

If making a concrete or paver labyrinth, I wouldn't go much over fifty feet in diameter. Otherwise, the labyrinth gets so big it looks like a parking lot. Most of our outdoor concrete Chartres labyrinths are the same exact size as in Chartres. The largest concrete labyrinth we have made is fifty-six feet across.

Lines and Paths

More important than the actual diameter of the labyrinth are the proportions, which should remain constant, as they have a specific symbolism. Using these proportions, you can calculate the measurements for sizes other than what I have included in this manual.

I have been approached a couple of times by people writing software that would determine the proportions of the labyrinth automatically by starting with the diameter. I don't know if they have been successful. It should be possible to start with any measurement, such as line or path or petal, and determine the rest, as they all relate to each other.

I first learned to draw the labyrinth in the summer of 1995 at the urging of an inner prompting. I had no background in mathematics or geometry. My goal was not to calculate but to draw.

My biggest breakthrough came with a discovery that unlocked the proportions. It had to do with drawing the lines. I tried to picture the stonecutters back at the dawn of the thirteenth century. The mason would have had a drawing floor, in which objects could be sketched out in flour dust for making templates. How would he have presented the lines?

In Chartres, the lines are three inches wide. The mason drawing the pattern couldn't have made a single line, which is how our eyes see it in drawings. You can't make that. A line has no dimensions. To make the pattern, he would have drawn two parallel lines, three inches apart, with the proper curved radius.

In other words, the line must be three-dimensional, with length and width (for a drawing) and thickness (for actual stone). To portray a line, I found, required drawing two lines, parallel, the distance between them determining the width.

This means that the inside of the line, closest to the center, would be based on a circle with a smaller radius than would the line on the outer edge, further from the center. Clearly, to be accurate, we must measure the lines in their full dimension.

Besides unlocking the proportions, this realization that lines have width became essential in how we made labyrinths. On canvas, for example, we invented a compass tool with two pencils, so that they always drew parallel lines, the area between which was painted.

Before drawing the circles, we marked out their proper locations along the vertical axis (on a strip of masking tape) with a notation that showed inner and outer, specifically, 3-i, 3-o, 4i, 4-o, etc.

When scoring a circular labyrinth pattern into concrete, we made similar marks, but had to cut the circles one at a time. As a result, we had to make twenty-four cuts to make twelve circles.

The paths, too, have specific proportions. I found that they relate to the lines in a proportion of 4.5 : 1. The line and path together comprise eleven units. The line is two of those units and the path is nine of those units, for a ratio of 9 : 2, also expressed as 4.5 : 1.

If you want 4" lines (the width of a standard brick), then the path would be 18" (4" x 4.5 = 18"). Or, say you have a path/line measurement of 15". Dividing by 11 gives a single unit of 1.36. The lines would be two of those (2.72") and the path nine of those (12.27"). I would round them off to 2¾" and 12¼".

The Proportions

<u>Center diameter</u>: One-fourth the diameter of the labyrinth, as measured from the outsides of the first and twelfth circles (excluding the lunations).

Petal diameter (outside line): One-third the diameter of the center circle.

Path width: One-third the outer diameter of the petal circle.

Lunation spacing: The same as the path width.

Line width: Divide the width of the path by 4.5, or, divide the path by 9 and multiply that result by two.

Petal crosses: The tips of the crosses at the ends of the petals are exactly one-half the distance from the center of the labyrinth to the outer first circle. In other words, they are located at one-half the length of the radius of 1-o (circle one, outer radius).

Lunation circle: The partial circle of the lunation and the width of the adjacent teeth have a proportion, not surprisingly, of 9:2. Just as the path was $^{9}/_{11}$ of the whole path/line unit, so the lunation circle is $^{9}/_{11}$ of the lunation unit, which is equal to the path width. That's a bit complicated to understand at first reading. The path is $^{9}/_{11}$ of the entire path/line unit. It subsequently becomes the whole unit for lunation spacing, of which the lunation circle is $^{9}/_{11}$.

Tooth height: The teeth are roughly the same height (from the inside of the 12th circle to the tip of the tooth, which includes the width of the 12th circle) as the diameter of the lunation circle. This achieves an eye-pleasing 1:1 ratio between the height of the teeth and the space between them.

Labrys width: The bow-tie-shaped figures formed by the back-to-back, 180-degree turns on the labyrinth are separated by a distance slightly wider than the width of the line (at Chartres, 3 1/4" vs. the line of 3").

Here are some examples of the proportions.

Size	12th Circle (outer)	1st Circle (outer)	Petal (outer)	Path & Lunation	Line Width
100'	97' 1"	24' 3"	8' 1"	2' 8⅜ "	7 3/16"
50'	48' 6½"	12' 1 11/16"	4' 9/16"	1' 4 1/16"	3⅝"
42' 3⅜"	41'½"	10' 3⅛"	3' 5 1/16"	1' 1 11/16"	3"
40'	38' 10"	9' 8½"	3' 2⅞"	1' 1"	2⅞"
35'	33' 11¾"	8' 5 15/16"	2' 10"	11 5/16"	2½"
30'	29' 1½"	7' 3⅜"	2' 5 3/16"	9¾"	2 3/16"

The third row of numbers reflects the actual size of the labyrinth in Chartres.

Here's a dilemma for me. The above figures were included in the original version of this book. But I don't actually use those figures anymore. I now use the following:

	Metric (mm)	Imperial (inches)
Diameter:	12,885	507⅜
Radius:	6,442.5	253 11/16
Center	3,120	122½
Center radius	1,560	61¼
One-half radius	780	30⅝
Line	75	3
Path	350	13¾
Path/Line unit	425	16¾
Tooth	207.5	8 3/16

Below are the measurements I use for locating the circles.

Circle	Inner / Outer (mm)		Inner / Outer (inches)	
1	1485	1560	58¼	61¼
2	1910	1985	75	78
3	2335	2410	91¾	94¾
4	2760	2835	108½	111½
5	3185	3260	125¼	128¼
6	3610	3685	142	145
7	4035	4110	158¾	161¾
8	4460	4535	175½	178½

9	4885	4960	192¼	195¼
10	5310	5385	209	212
11	5735	5810	225¾	228¾
12	6160	(6235)	242½	(245½)
T	6442.5		(253 11/16)	

Accuracy

If you plug in the exact proportions (one-third of this, one-fourth of that) and multiply them by their appropriate multiples, you will find that they don't quite add up. That's because these are all averages, for which there is a small amount of variation. If the lines are 3" then the path should be 13½" for a total path/line of 16½". But if you look in the table above, the path/line unit totals 16 11/16". That's rather clumsy, so I usually use 16¾" (second set of numbers). Since there are 22 lines, adding 1/16" totals 1⅜". If you want the labyrinth to remain exactly 42' 3⅜" in diameter, then you must find somewhere else, usually the center, to subtract this amount in a way that won't be noticed.

And even these numbers don't please me. I show the path as 350 mm. Numerous values found on the internet use 343 mm. The *pes manualis,* Scarlet's foot measure, is 354 mm. Surely he made the paths one foot wide. Yet to do so increases the labyrinth diameter by too much. Maybe, in the end, to get everything to balance out, he, too, had to fudge a little. I sure hope so.

As a rule of thumb, the diameter of the labyrinth (not counting lunations) is approximately 30 times the width of the path/line unit. This is helpful when laying out with rocks, in which case the actual proportions for the line and path don't apply exactly.

If you space the circles 3' apart, for example, then that is the value for the path/line unit, in which case the labyrinth will be approximately 90' in diameter. Checking it, we find the 22 path/line units across the diameter would equal 66' (22 x 3'). They represent three-fourths of the diameter of the labyrinth (not counting the lunations). So to find out the remaining one-fourth, we divide 66' by three, to get 22'. Everything adds up to 88' which is 2' different from the estimate of 90'.

How accurate is that? About 98%. Just a rule of thumb.

Additionally, the length of the path is roughly 20 times the diameter of the labyrinth. So the length of the path for a 90' labyrinth would equal 1,800'. That would make a round trip, in to the center and back out, 3,600', or five-eighths of a mile.

Look at the overall proportions of the labyrinth. The center is one-fourth the diameter, the petals are one-third of the center, and the paths arone-third of the petals. The paths, therefore, are ¼ x ⅓ x ⅓ = $^1/_{36}{}^{th}$ of the diameter of the labyrinth, not counting the lunations. The path width, you will remember, is also the lunation spacing.

So let's say that you have an outdoor labyrinth 48' in diameter, and you want to add lunations. Divide that diameter by thirty-six to get 16". Space the lunations 16" apart, and you will be close. You will need to fudge the last few to make it look just right. If you find the circumference of a 48' circle and divide by 114 lunations (including the entrance), you get 15.87". So the rule of thumb is quite close.

Making temporary or informal labyrinths, these rules of thumb should suit you just fine. If you are making a serious canvas or permanent labyrinth, then you will want to make your calculations in advance to see exactly where and how the fudging takes place. Fudging is also necessary to draw the petals and lunations, as we shall see later.

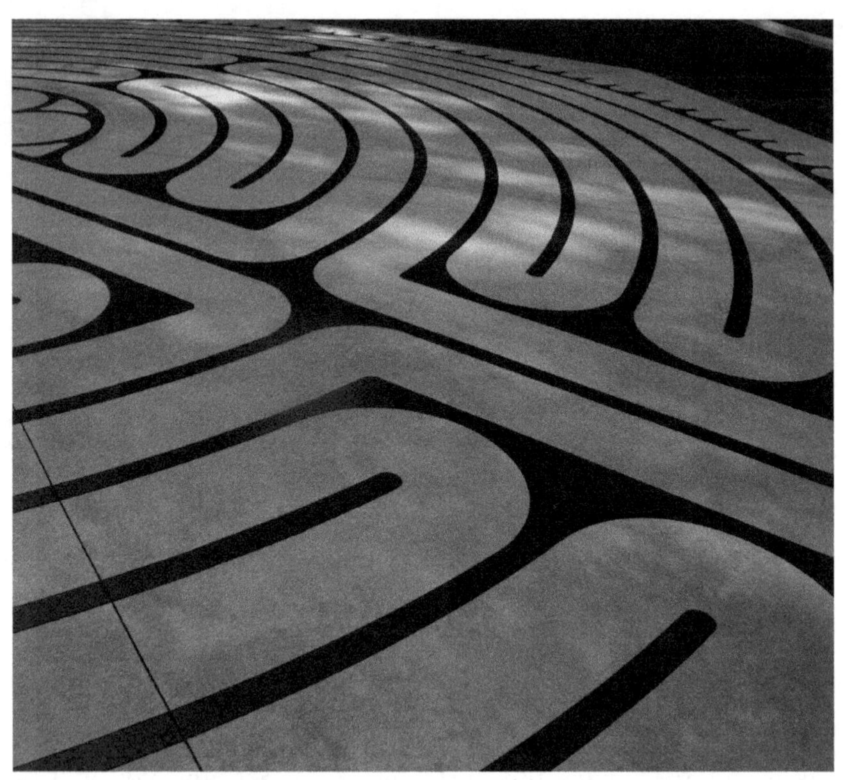

Chartres labyrinth at Kanuga Retreat Center, Hendersonville, North Carolina

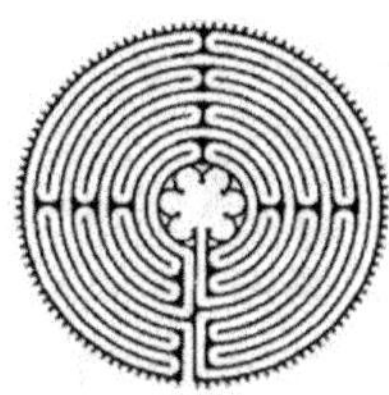

Symbolism

Sacred geometry is the quest to understand the act of Creation by studying the numbers and proportions exhibited in nature, thereby revealing the underlying lawfulness. When I give talks about sacred geometry, some people stay away because they are math phobic. But it really has little to do with mathematics, which is a technical language used to describe geometry and not geometry itself, which is the drawing of shapes and figures.

There are four assumptions in sacred geometry

1. Divine Maker

A Divine Hand created the physical world. In the past few hundred years, this had been questioned by science, and made politically incorrect by extreme fundamentalism. Nevertheless, it has been the predominant assumption for thousands of years.

2. Number and proportion

Creation was made according to number and proportion, which can be expressed through geometry. Since this geometry emanated from the Divine Mind, it's sacred. Hence, sacred geometry.

3. Discovering lawfulness

By studying nature, we can discover the lawfulness that lies behind Creation. Plato said it is the search for "the eternally true." For example, the Pythagorean Theorem expresses a truth about the nature of right triangles which applies to all triangles that have a square corner. It's universally true.

4. Creating like God

Once we understand the lawfulness and have a grasp of the geometry, we can then use that knowledge to create in ways consistent with nature, just as the Creator did. Virtually all temples and sacred structures (with exceptions in modern times) were built using sacred geometry. The labyrinth and Chartres Cathedral are no exception.

The imitation of Creation is a spiritual and devotional practice that reveals truths about ourselves. In Michael Schneider's book *A Beginner's Guide to Constructing the Universe* (see www.constructingtheuniverse.com), John Michel wrote in the Introduction:

> *As soon as you enter upon the world of sacred, symbolic, or philosophical geometry – from your first thoughtful construction of a circle with the circumference divided into its six natural parts – your mind is opened to new influences that stimulate and refine it. You begin to see, as never before, the wonderfully patterned beauty of Creation. You see true artistry, far above any human contrivance. This indeed is the very source of art. By contact with it your aesthetic senses are heightened and set upon the firm basis of truth. Beyond the obvious pleasure of contemplating works of nature – the Many –is the delight that comes through the philosophical study of geometry, of moving toward the presence of the One."*

The quality of numbers

Over the centuries, certain numbers and proportions have taken on meanings, which can be incorporated into temples and churches and other structures to express the desired symbolism. Thus, numbers have a qualitative aspect in addition to their quantitative and descriptive functions.

Numbers make a difference. They affect us in various ways. Robert Gilbert, a sacred geometry teacher, states:

> *"Much more than 'symbolic' patterns of art and philosophy, the true science of Sacred Geometry allows direct, practical access to the spiritual and material forces of creation."*

When creating a labyrinth, it's not just a frivolous activity. It involves deep meaning and important aspects that will affect those walking the labyrinth.

All numbers have meaning, but some stand out for their importance and usefulness. Here are a few.

Three, in Christian symbolism, refers to the Trinity, and more broadly spirit, holiness, and the soul.

Four represents the physical world, the body, time and space, the mundane.

Ideally, the full person integrates both of these aspects, being fully spiritual and fully physical, which can be done in two ways:

$$3 + 4 = 7$$

$$3 \times 4 = 12$$

Seven and twelve are the most mystical of all numbers. In the book of Revelation there are seven veils, seven horns, seven, seven, seven, everywhere. We find seven gifts of the spirit, seven vices and virtues, and so forth. Twelve is also significant, as in the number of disciples, tribes of Israel, signs of the zodiac, months in the year, and more.

Take a moment to look at the pattern of the Chartres labyrinth.

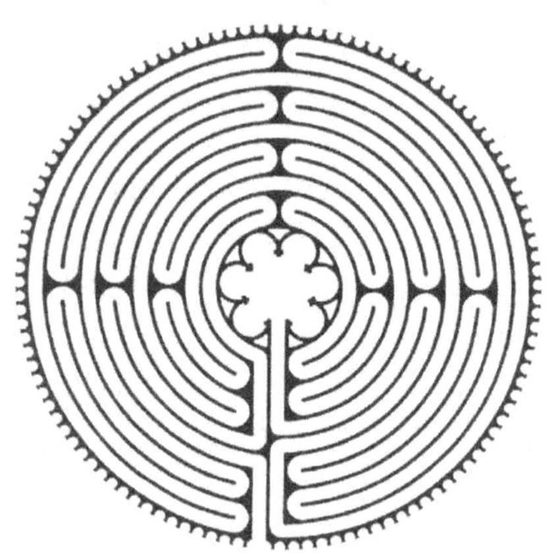

There are *twelve* concentric circles, forming eleven paths. (Eleven stands for sin, excess, inadequacy, confusion, worldliness – giving us a hint why the labyrinth serves as a metaphor for our path through life.)

The back-to-back turns, called labryses, divide the labyrinth into *four* quadrants (the world), forming a cross (suffering, sacrifice). Each quadrant has *four* turns on the vertical axis and *three* turns on the horizontal axis, hence, *seven* turns in each quadrant for a total of 28, considered a lunar number.

The lunations, the partial circles around the perimeter, number 112, or four symbolic lunar months (4 x 28 = 112). In the iconography of Chartres Cathedral, solar symbolism refers to Jesus and lunar to the Virgin Mary.

In manuscripts, labyrinth illustrations almost always accompanied either the topic of Easter (determined by the lunar calendar, being the first Sunday after the first full moon after the spring equinox) or signs of the zodiac, which represented the passing of the seasons and time (our journey through life).

Go back to the previous discussion about the proportions of the labyrinth elements to each other. They were one-fourth and one-third, again incorporating the numbers that add up to seven. In the cathedral itself, there are seven bays in the nave (archways between the nave and the aisles). The center of the labyrinth divides them into four and three bays.

Sacred geometers concentrate on the numbers one through ten, which in turn generate all other numbers. Often they are expressed as a triangle of ten dots called the tetraktys (below).

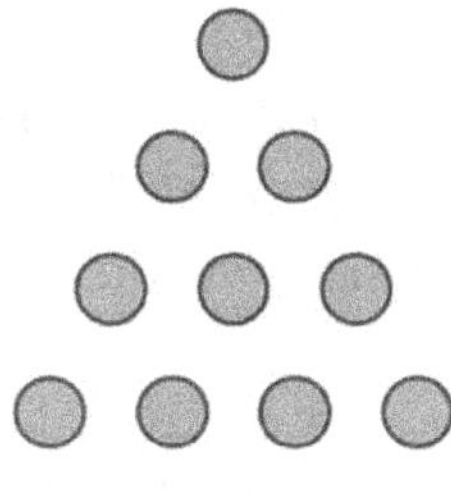

All of the numbers in the tetraktys generate other numbers, such as 2 x 3 = 6 or 3 x 3 = 9, with one exception: the number seven. It neither generates nor is generated by any of the other numbers. It stands alone, with no offspring. As such, it has historically been called "the virgin." Is it any surprise, then, that the number seven is so predominant in a labyrinth and a cathedral dedicated to Mary?

Divide the tetraktys numbers into 360 (the number of degrees in a circle), and you get even numbers (180, 120, 90, etc.) except for seven. It yields 51.42857. (Isn't that the angle between the side and base of the Great Pyramid?) Seven stands alone in its properties.

As we will soon see, the petals are also based on a geometry of seven, placing Mary in the center of the world/labyrinth, just as has been done with the cathedral itself, God's home on earth. Interestingly, the center of the labyrinth also represents heaven, the end of our spiritual journey (after completing our labyrinthine path through life). That Mary will be there waiting for us was a very strong and influential belief in the Middle Ages.

The church had long overplayed its hand in sin and damnation such that almost everyone feared they would be condemned and never make it to paradise. Then along came the adoration of Mary, who would lobby on one's behalf, say a favorable word to her Son, and make heaven possible. Devotion to Mary was promulgated by influential champions such as Bernard of Clairvaux and the monastic community. This helps to explain why the vast majority of churches were dedicated to Notre Dame, Our Lady.

There are other important symbolic proportions in the labyrinth, each tantalizingly close yet still slightly off. For example, I originally thought the length of the lunation teeth was determined by making a geometric figure called the *vesica piscis* from the lunation circles, but that turned out not to be the case. The tooth is slightly shorter than that, apparently in order to incorporate another important proportion within the labyrinth: the golden mean.

If the center is one-fourth the diameter of the labyrinth from 12-0, then the ratio of the center to one side would be 1 : 1½. Remember the paths total three-fourths of the diameter, and the center one-fourth. So one side would equal half of three-fourths, or one and one-half fourths for the paths and one-fourth for the center, for the ratio above, which can be written 1 : 1.5.

If we measure to the tip of the lunation, however, rather than to the twelfth circle, the ratio changes, to 1 : 1.62 which is known as the golden mean, an important and mystical proportion expressed throughout the natural world.

Similarly, there are a total of twenty-two path/line units across the diameter of the labyrinth. The center comes very close to equalling seven path/line units. The fraction $^{22}/_{7}$ was the value used for *pi* in the middle ages.

Pi is an irrational and transcendent number which represents the relationship between the diameter and the circumference of a circle. Historically, calculating *pi* was a favorite pastime of mathematicians. It's a non-repeating number that goes on forever, generally rounded off to four decimal places: 3.1416.

The fraction $^{22}/_{7}$ has a decimal value of 3.1428. The error is only .0012 or four hundredths of one percent.

The path width and lunations give another approximation of *pi*. Remember we pointed out that the path width is equal to one-third of the petals, which are one-third of the center, which is one-fourth the diameter of the labyrinth. That means the path width is ⅓ x ⅓ x ¼ , or $^{1}/_{36}$th the diameter of the labyrinth. We have already noted that the width of the path equals the size of a lunation (circle and tooth). There would be 114 lunations around the perimeter of the labyrinth, except that one was removed for the entrance path – but the space is still there. Hence, in path/width units, we have values for both the diameter and the circumference, 36 and 114 respectively. Decimally, the fraction $^{114}/_{36}$ yields a value of 3.1667 (error: $^{25}/_{1000}$ or approximately three-fourths of one percent).

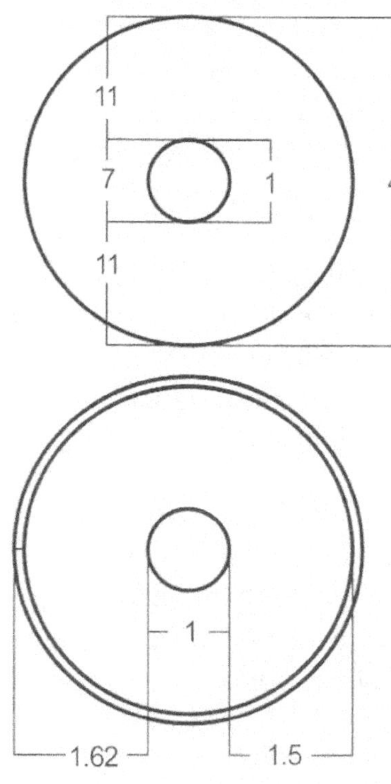

Incorporating the value of *pi* and other such relationships is an ancient practice. I've read that the width of the lintel (horizontal) stones at Stonehenge equal the diameter of a circle whose circumference determines their length, hence representing the proportion of *pi*.

So, as you can see, in sacred geometry the measurements and proportions hold a lot of symbolism and meaning. To arrive at these auspicious proportions, we must do a little fudging. In one case we may measure from the outside of a circle, and for another from the inside, or somewhere within the line. This is almost certainly intentional. If everything were rigidly precise, then there would be no mystery, no surprise. The language of spirituality is not literal. I often wonder what other relationships were obvious to the builder which we, with our modern minds, do not appreciate.

The secret of the petals

If you draw a circle with a compass and don't change the setting, you can draw six more circles that will be exactly tangent to the center circle.

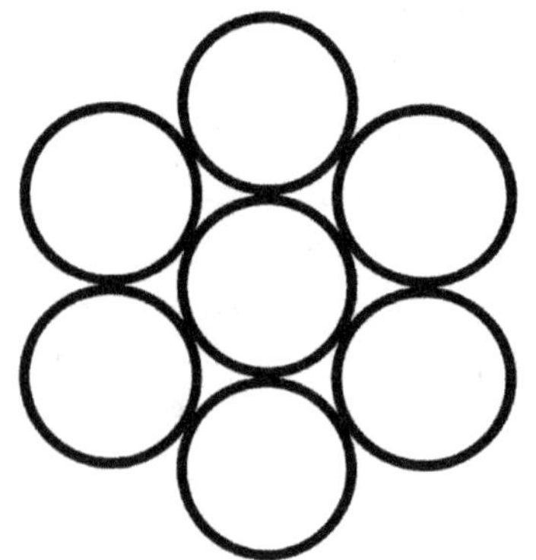

If you then draw a larger circle around the whole figure, you would have the basis for the center petals in the labyrinth. Note that each of the individual circles would have a diameter of one-third the entire figure, which is exactly the case for the petals in the labyrinth.

But wait, if the circles are that size, how is there room for an entrance? The solution is ingenious: each petal overlaps its neighboring petal by the thickness of the line. The circles remain the same size, they are just rearranged. This opens up space for the entrance without reducing the size of the petals.

When I discovered this, I was very proud of myself. Later, I found that John James copied my discovery and published it ten years earlier! Oh, well, at least it gave me confirmation. One of my most nostalgic drawings is my first drawing of the center petals. (The petal crosses were not yet revealed.)

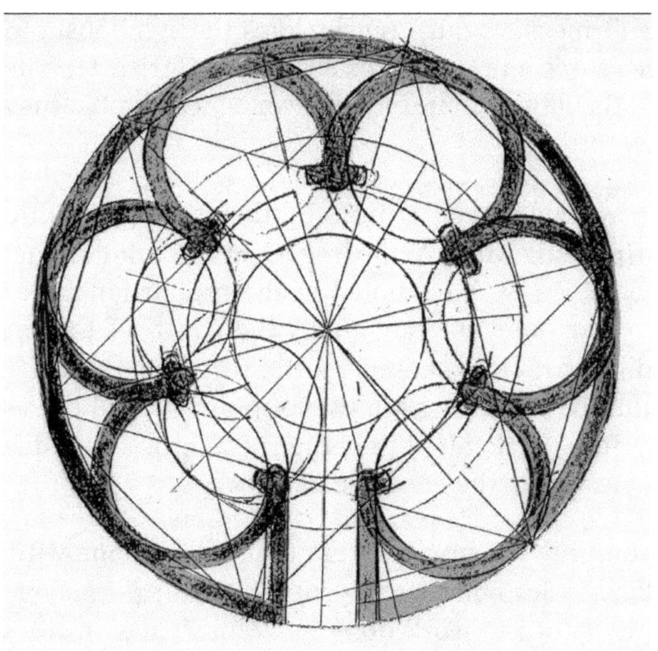

This geometry is also why the labyrinth is *not* based on an invisible 13-pointed star. In such case, the path would equal half the diameter of a petal. The petals would thus each be $^2/_{13}$ when they are actually $^2/_{12}$ or $^1/_6$. We already have seen that the path equals one-third the diameter of the petal. A 13-pointed star would reduce the size of the petals to make room for the entrance, rather than overlapping them.

I have measured the entrance very closely, and the 13-pointed star is off by some six or seven percent, which would be a huge error. Consider the difference of the fractions:

1/12 = .0833333
1/13 = .0769230

The difference is .0064103, which, divided by .0833333 gives an error of 7.69%. Divided by .0769230 the error is 8.33%.

The idea of the 13-pointed star was published by Keith Critchlow in 1972 and is still being repeated in some books–but it's erroneous. In fact, Keith Critchlow himself, with whom I have studied sacred geometry on two occasions, admits that "it doesn't measure out," but he likes the symbolism in which thirteen represents twelve disciples plus Christ. He misses the fact that the labyrinth numbers invoke Mary, not Jesus and the disciples.

Since the petals overlap five times, then the path width should be five times the width of the line, right? Not quite. That would be too easy. As we have noted in the proportions, the path is equal to four and one-half times the width of the line. This slight discrepancy is caused by the fact that the half-crosses that flank the entrance path do not point toward the center of the labyrinth, as do all of the other petal crosses. Instead, they remain parallel to the entrance path.

If you multiply the investigation that I have done with regard to the labyrinth to include the entire cathedral, you get an idea of the scope of the work done by John James in his seminal work, *The Contractors of Chartres*, which changed the way we understand Gothic construction. He is now engaged in his life work, a similar study of 1,500 Gothic structures in the Paris Basin in a multivolume collection called *The Ark of God*. This incredible body of work is being made available on the website www.creationofgothic.org.

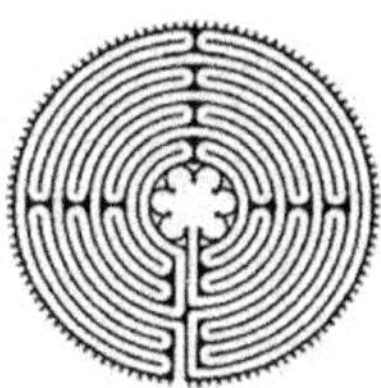

Site and Orientation

Before we can start drawing, we must determine some of the parameters and give ourselves some guidelines. For that reason, I more often say "laying out" the labyrinth rather than drawing it.

The first task is to establish the site, size, and orientation of the labyrinth. (These features can also determine the best pattern or design.) This applies only to permanent labyrinths, as only size is required for portable ones made on canvas (and the direction of the seams).

There are numerous ways to determine the orientation of the labyrinth.

<u>The architecture</u>
In Chartres, the labyrinth is in the nave with the entrance facing the western entrance. For this reason, Christian labyrinths are often laid out to face west, so that the walker faces away from the setting sun, darkness, death, and enters facing east (the direction of the rising sun, hope, light, the risen Son).

In actuality, Chartres is an exception to this rule. In Chartres, the orientation of the cathedral is something like 46 degrees off in comparison to the cardinal directions, resulting in a southwest-northeast orientation. Other Gothic cathedrals are more directly west-east.

While many esoteric possibilities have been theorized to explain this anomaly, it may have resulted from a far more mundane circumstance. Archeological digs in the plaza in the 1980s showed that the cathedral is consistent with the street grid of the original Roman city that once occupied that hilltop. The early Christians likely built a small temple on a cheap lot tucked against the wall, facing the street.

Subsequent churches on the site were built on top of the original, enlarging it many times but retaining the same orientation.

If a modern church is built so that it doesn't face west, then the labyrinth is more likely to follow the orientation of the church than to impose some unnatural direction upon it.

Dowsing

I cover dowsing in more detail in *The Labyrinth Revival.* Most people associate dowsers with forked sticks seeking out water sources. But modern dowsing is much more than that. In essence, dowsing consults the site itself, which is to say, the earth and its discarnate entities, to determine the proper location, size, and orientation.

By doing so, dowsers believe they maximize the power and energy of the labyrinth, which come from the earth. In contrast, the Christian tradition holds that the power comes not from the earth or even the labyrinth itself, but from the act of walking it.

On pilgrimage the power of one's experience doesn't come from the path one walks, although it's an important component of the overall experience. I don't find the two different approaches mutually exclusive. Each is proper within its own context, and occasionally, both apply.

Astrological significance

Many ancient and megalithic sites were built so that on a certain day of the year, such as the spring equinox or the summer solstice, the rays of the sun enter a special chamber or hit a particular point. I have never built a labyrinth with such an orientation, but it's certainly possible.

I have read a few mistaken theories about the light from the rose window in Chartres Cathedral hitting the labyrinth on a certain day. Another theory suggests that were the western wall hinged at its base, the rose window would exactly cover the labyrinth. Not so. These are urban myths that I once repeated myself, but have proved to be erroneous.

Geographical feature

When entering the labyrinth, it is pleasant to be facing a mountain peak or a tree or some other geographical feature. Sometimes there's an outdoor altar (or one can be built along with the labyrinth). There could be other reasons why the landscape itself favors a certain orientation.

Feels right

Often I stand or sit on a potential site until I get a feel for it. The details of the labyrinth emerge organically rather than formulating in my rational mind. In a way, being intuitive is like dowsing, without the implements. I prefer to believe that time is not linear (it all exists at once), so that in actuality, I'm remembering the future, with the labyrinth occupying that site. (I ascribe the same concept to people buying houses, who choose the one they buy because, unknowingly, they remember living there in the future and so feel right at home.)

Presence of water

Hundreds of stone labyrinths surround the Baltic Sea, some dating back 500 years or more. They have been attributed to fishermen, who walked them to encourage favorable winds and good catches. In such case, the entrance of the labyrinth usually faces the sea, so that the fishermen could come out of the labyrinth and head directly to their ships. (The bad luck trolls, still in the labyrinth, would be left behind.)

Predetermined

In many cases the site of the labyrinth offers no alternative. For example, being in a small courtyard. Public labyrinths often face the sidewalk or area of access. It's important for the labyrinth to be inviting, to beckon people to come and walk. If a person can't easily see the entrance, then he or she may decide to pass up the opportunity to walk it.

Follow instructions

The labyrinth can be part of a larger landscaping project, such as a healing garden beside a hospital. In such case, the architect may have drawn up plans and determined the orientation of the labyrinth. Sometimes, feeling the design could be improved, I have made suggestions which have then been incorporated into the design. The architect may not have been aware of consciously orienting the labyrinth in a certain way.

Sacred geometry

A sacred space has certain features, including a specific perimeter, one or more entrances, and a defined center or altar space. The labyrinth has all of these, in and of itself, but sometimes the perimeter or entrance can be extended outward to create a whole sacred precinct with benches and lighting and water features. Here again, the overall design may affect the presentation of the labyrinth.

The orientation of the labyrinth shouldn't be random or haphazard. It should address some aspect of the site, the architecture, or the intended use.

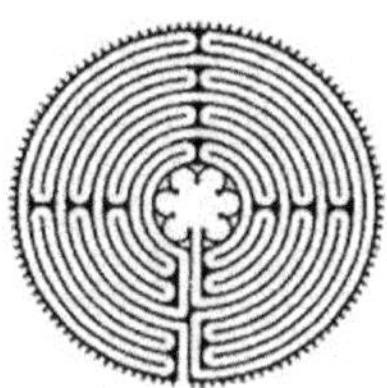

A General Overview

As you have seen, many important considerations go into the construction of a labyrinth, and specifically, the Chartres Labyrinth. Before describing each element of the labyrinth in detail, let's consider the basic strategy that will make this complicated design more accessible, a general overview of the process itself.

One of my favorite books shows extremely ornate Islamic architectural patterns, and then, step by step, how to start with circles and form octagons and continue elaborating until the final pattern is achieved. Making a labyrinth is much the same.

After establishing the size, location, and orientation, we mark out the horizontal and vertical axes. (The vertical axis is parallel to the entrance paths while the horizontal axis goes side to side.) Outdoors, I generally do this by using stakes and string. Indoors, if making a labyrinth out of masking tape, string can also be used, by simply taping the ends to the floor. On canvas or concrete, I lay down a strip of masking tape along each of the axes. Later, I will make all of my guide marks on these strips, so they can be easily removed.

Using your precalculated measurements, mark on the vertical axis the location of the twelve circles that will comprise the labyrinth. I make two marks, for the inside and outside of the circles and label them accordingly: 1-i, 1-o, 2-i, 2-o (i = inner, o = outer), etc.

Next, I mark the entrance paths, which involves locating the three straight lines that enclose the two entrance paths. Then, using whatever sort of compass has been devised, lay out the twelve concentric circles. By marking the entrance paths first, we avoid making the circles where they don't belong, as they would just have to be removed.

Once the circles are made, the details come into play, specifically, the labryses (180 degree turns that give the labyrinth its cruciform appearance), the central petals, and the lunations (the perimeter arcs). Taking one element at a time, we can complete the task of laying out the labyrinth.

The techniques used in laying out the labyrinth will vary, depending on the medium. If using masking tape on the floor, mistakes are no problem, as the tape can be removed. The same with placing stones on the ground. If painting the grass, it's harder, but the grass can be cut or pulled out to eliminate a mistake. On canvas, more precision is needed, as it's very hard to erase extraneous lines from the canvas. Drawing on concrete with indelible markers, all extraneous lines must be avoided.

The ideal, therefore, is to use some means to indicated where to start and stop each circle. If painting on grass, yardsticks or pieces of cardboard (or a volunteer standing there) can be used to mark the stopping points so that you don't overextend the lines.

Each of these steps will be covered in detail in the coming sections. While it may sound a bit overwhelming at first, by proceeding one step at a time a good result may be realized. The process is summarized in the drawings below.

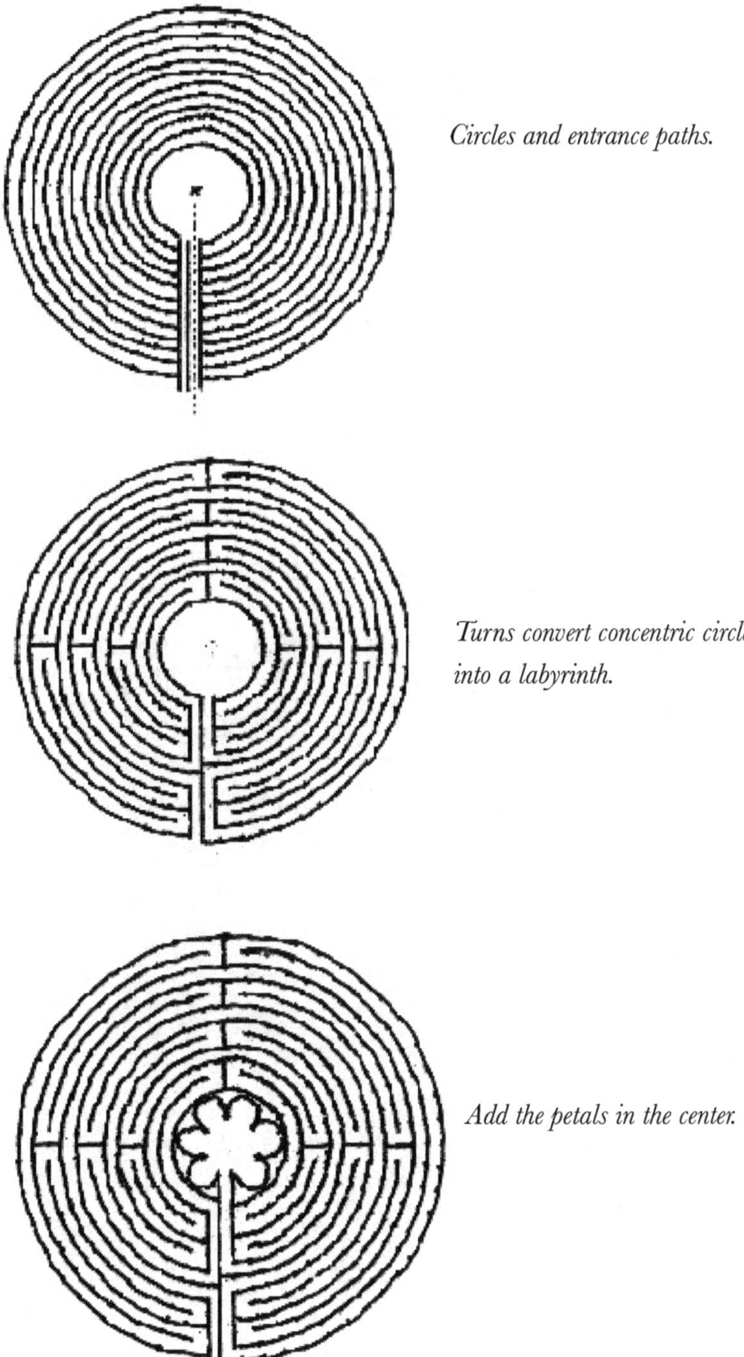

Circles and entrance paths.

Turns convert concentric circles into a labyrinth.

Add the petals in the center.

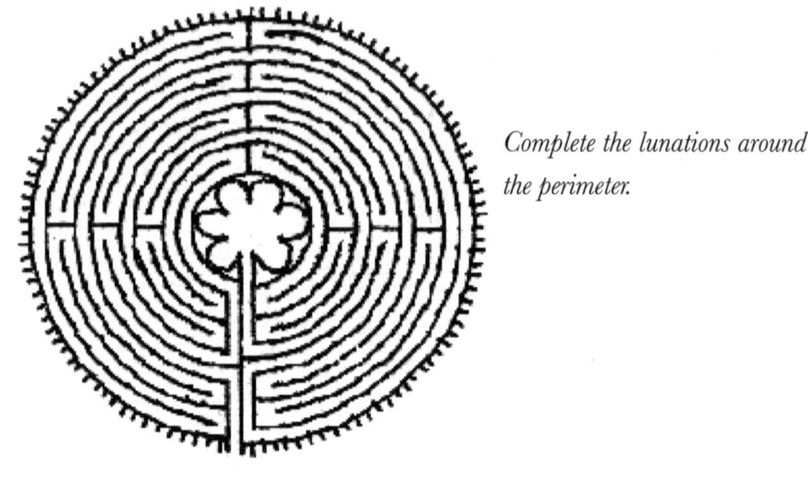

Complete the lunations around the perimeter.

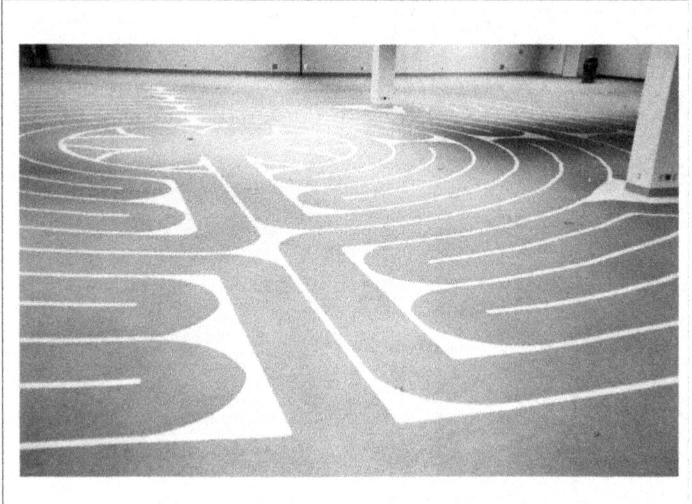

One-hundred-foot diameter masking tape labyrinth with detours that go around the pillars. Used for one evening (New Year's Eve, 1996) and then removed. Walked by more than 2,000 people (hence the large size).

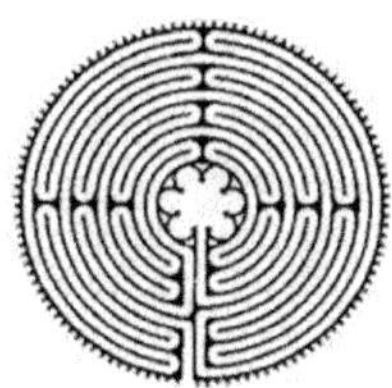

The Circles

Preparation

Finally, time to start drawing. At this point you have done the following:

1. Established the desired site and orientation of the labyrinth

2. Prepared the site as necessary. If concrete, it could mean power washing or acid etching to clean the surface and open the pores. If grass, it may mean cutting the grass first so the paint will last as long as possible before the next mowing. When mowing the labyrinth into the grass, let it grow long first. If canvas, you would have had it sewn together and now held in place to keep it from moving.

3. Ordered the materials, be they stones, masking tape, cans of paint, etc.

4. Assembled the tools. You will need tape measures, a compass, and more (spray paint, paint wands, whatever).

5. Marked out the guide rope with the specific measurements.

6. Arranged for the workers, given them instructions, blessed them, the tools, and the project. Have water and snacks available.

7. Have a drawing of the labyrinth to refer to and to show inquisitive lookers on. We sometimes put up posters explaining what a labyrinth is and how people will be able to use it. Review the instructions and begin.

Marking the center

If outdoors, drive a stake into the ground where the center of the labyrinth will be. If on canvas, floor, or concrete, put down a piece of tape with an "X" marking the center point.

How you find the center of an existing piece of concrete depends on the shape. If it's square or rectangular, measure across the diagonals. Where they cross will be the center. For a circle, you can bisect two random segments drawn across the circle. Where they cross is the center (see diagram).

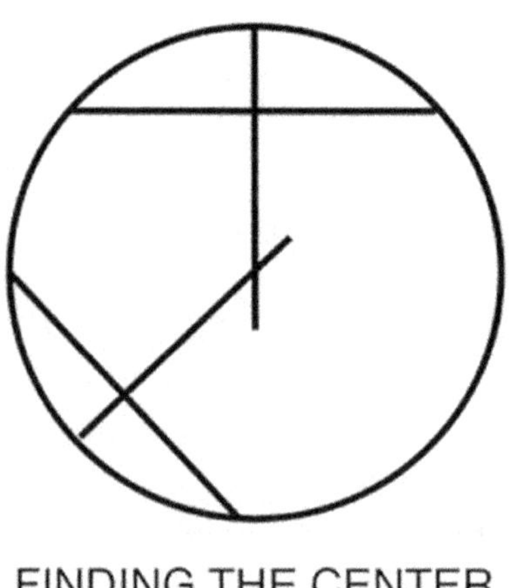

FINDING THE CENTER OF A CIRCLE

Laying out the axes

I am using the word *axes* as the plural of axis. It could be confused with the plural for the word ax, especially since the back-to-back turns are called labryses, which invoke the double headed ax of Minoan lore. These axes are just vertical and horizontal guidelines, not weapons.

By laying out the vertical axis first, you establish the desired orientation—what direction you want to face when entering the labyrinth. If outside, I use stakes and mason's string to mark the axes.

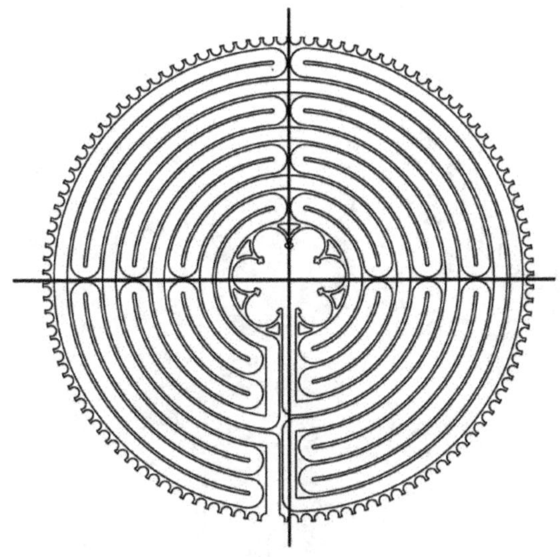

When marking the axis, step back a pace or two so the stakes don't interfere with drawing the labyrinth. Put the first stake into the ground. Tie one end of the mason's string to the stake and walk to what will be the top of the labyrinth. The center of the labyrinth should already be marked, so make sure the vertical axis goes directly across the center point and out to a second stake.

If you have several volunteers, you can use the same method to mark the axis with masking tape. Have two people extend a long tape measure (or mason's line, stretched taut) and hold it in place while someone else lays down a strip of masking tape right beside it. One edge of the tape measure should line up with the center point. In that way, one edge of the tape will do the same. Use a pen to draw an arrow to indicate which edge of the tape is on the axis.

In our studio we had long straightedges which we used for this purpose. We made them by going to a company that sold supplies for awning makers. They had aluminum channel for awnings as long as twenty-four feet. We cut them down to eighteen- and twelve-foot lengths.

Having established the vertical axis, we must now mark out the horizontal axis. This is done by making a line (string, tape, rocks) perpendicular to the vertical axis that runs through the center point.

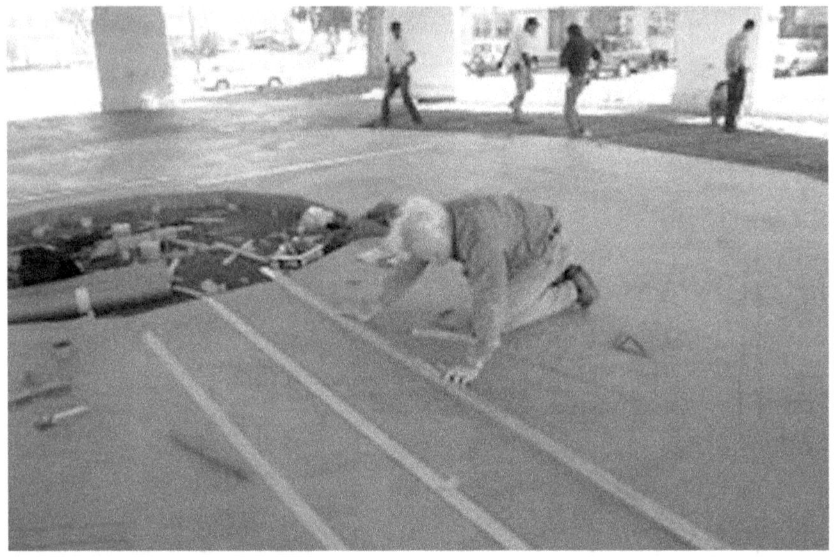

Here I'm laying out the entrance lines as described above with a long straightedge.

Geometrically, we usually establish the perpendicular (horizontal) axis by triangulating from two points along the vertical axis that are equidistant from the center point of the labyrinth.

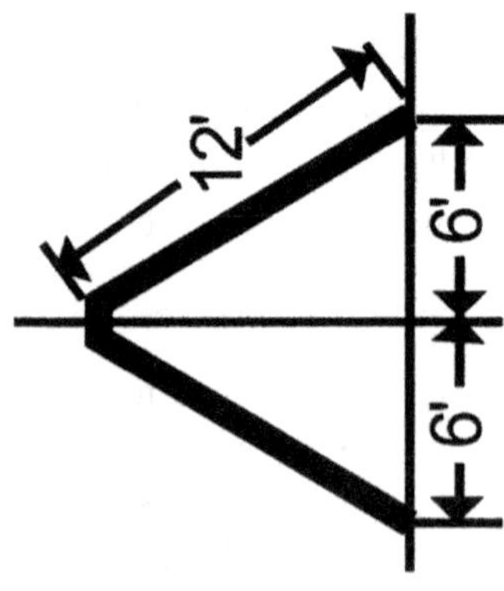

As in the diagram, mark a point 6' (or any other distance you choose) from the center point in each direction on the vertical axis (6' above the center and 6' below the center). We put a 12' straightedge at each of those marks. The point at which these two straightedges meet, thereby forming an equilateral isosceles triangle, marks the horizontal axis.

(I put a piece of masking tape there and make a “V” by tracing along the straightedges.)

Repeat the same procedure in the other direction, marking both the left and right location of the horizontal axis. Then use those points to lay out the horizontal axis.

Yes, there are electronic tools which will do this quite readily. I have one that’s made for laying tile, which needs to be accurate lest the error multiply from one end of the floor to the other. I also have a laser level with a side laser that indicates the perpendicular. There are other geometric methods for making a perpendicular (some of which use circles), but I find triangulation the easiest.

Geometry was invented in ancient Egypt, where the Nile flooded every spring, causing them to mark anew the various property lines each year. The meaning of the word comes from *geo* (earth) and *metry* (measurement). They used knotted ropes, which I demonstrate in my labyrinth master classes. (I call them ancient Egyptian geometry computers.)

From our basic geometry lessons we remember that a triangle with sides of three, four, and five will form a square corner (a right triangle). If making a labyrinth outdoors you may have a guide rope with the spacing for the circles marked on it. You can use that to form a right triangle.

Along the vertical axis, mark four units. Have someone hold the rope there. Then, count out five units and have someone hold the rope there. Finally, count out three more units and put that point in the center, on the vertical axis, at the point where you began.

Holding firm at the two points along the vertical axis, have the person holding the rope at the five unit mark pull the rope taut. It will form a right triangle as shown in the diagram below, thereby giving you the perpendicular.

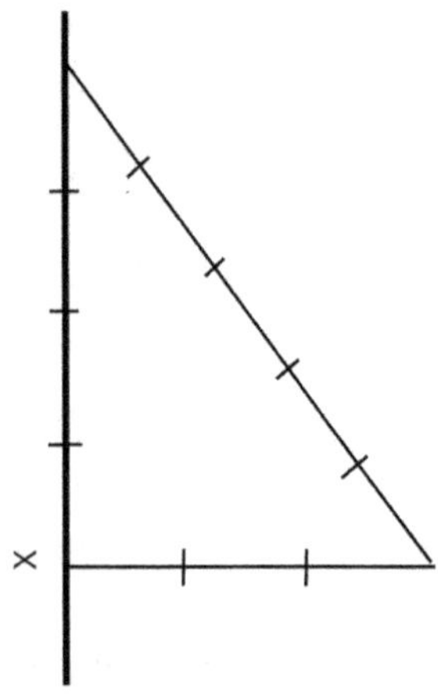

Left: 3-4-5 right triangle giving the perpendicular to the vertical axis at point "X"

Suppose you made a 4-4-5 triangle instead, what shape would it give? An equilateral isosceles triangle that forms the profile of the Great Pyramid! That was easy. Must have been a very large rope!

Frankly, when making temporary labyrinths, I just eyeball the horizontal axis. If you have the vertical axis in place and the center marked, have two people stretch a string along the proposed horizontal axis. Look down at the intersection where the two strings cross. All four angles should be the same. If the horizontal string isn't perpendicular, two angles with the vertical string will be larger and two smaller. Adjust the string until the angles look equal and you should be very close to perpendicular.

Marking the circle spacing

If you are drawing on canvas or concrete, mark out the circle spacing on the masking tape axes. Measure outward from the center and mark the location of the 12 circles. A short cut is to mark the circles only on the vertical axis at the entrance, since once started, a circle should need no further mark until it returns to the starting point. However, if you mark the circles on all four axes (top, bottom, left, right) they are helpful in verifying that your circles are accurate and not spiraling.

Number from the inside of the circle outward. There's nothing magic about that direction. You could number from the outside in, but you will be measuring the circles from the center outward, so it's easier to number them in ascending order.

If you are working precisely and plan to paint or stain the lines, then mark both the inner and outer circles as I have previously indicated (1-i, 1-o, etc.) Technically, you don't need to mark 12-o, as there are lunations there. However, I tend to mark 12-o for reference, and also the circle for the tips of the lunations. (When making the labyrinth on concrete, we use our taping machine to make an outer circle that delineates the ends of the lunation teeth.)

Remember you are marking the radius, not the diameter. So if the center is 10', the mark for 1-o (outer) will be 60" (which is five feet, half of the center diameter of ten feet). The mark for 1-i, toward the center, will be one line width less than 1-o (say, 57"). Make the rest of your marks outward by alternately measuring path and line widths.

If you are placing rocks on the ground, spray painting the grass, or making a temporary masking tape labyrinth, you don't need to mark the circle spacing on the axes. Instead, make a guide rope and mark the spacing on that. It's best to use rope that won't stretch (nylon works well), or chain or cable. At the end of the guide rope make a loop that will go around the center post.

As you don't need both inner and outer circle measurements, the circle spacing will be the equivalent of one path/line unit. To calculate this, divide your desired size (diameter) by four. One of those fourths will be the center. The remaining three-fourths will comprise the lines and paths. Take the value of those three-fourths and divide by twenty-two (eleven path/line units on each side, measuring outward from the center circle).

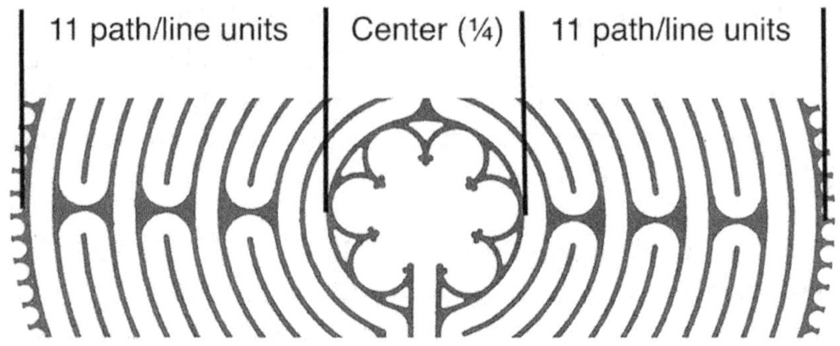

Center = ¼ the diameter. The remaining ¾ = the 22 path/line units.

For example, say the labyrinth is 40' in diameter (not counting the lunations). The center, being one-fourth of the diameter, will be 10'. The twenty-two path/line units take up the remaining 30'. Dividing 30' (360") by twenty-two we get 16.36" (call it 16⅜"). That would be your spacing. If you want to include the lunations in the 40' diameter, divide by twenty-three (rather than twenty-two) for the path/line unit, which will give you spacing of 15.65" (15⅝") , as the teeth are close to one half of the path/line unit. Thus, the teeth would be approximately 7³⁄₁₆" tall.

I like to use two-inch-wide masking tape to mark the circle spacing on the guide rope, so that there's no mistaking where to put down the rocks or tape.

If you want to practice making the Chartres labyrinth, make one that's 10' in diameter with ¾" masking tape and follow all of these instructions in miniature. Once you have it down, you can make a Chartres labyrinth of any size.

STOP! Don't draw or lay out the circles yet. There's more you need to know first, about the entrance and the turns. They influence where you do and don't draw the circles.

Marking the entrance paths

I have seen many Chartres labyrinths drawn wrong by putting the middle straight line (between the entrance paths) directly on the axis. If you do this, then the entrance path into the center will be offset to the right, which looks weird and throws off the petals.

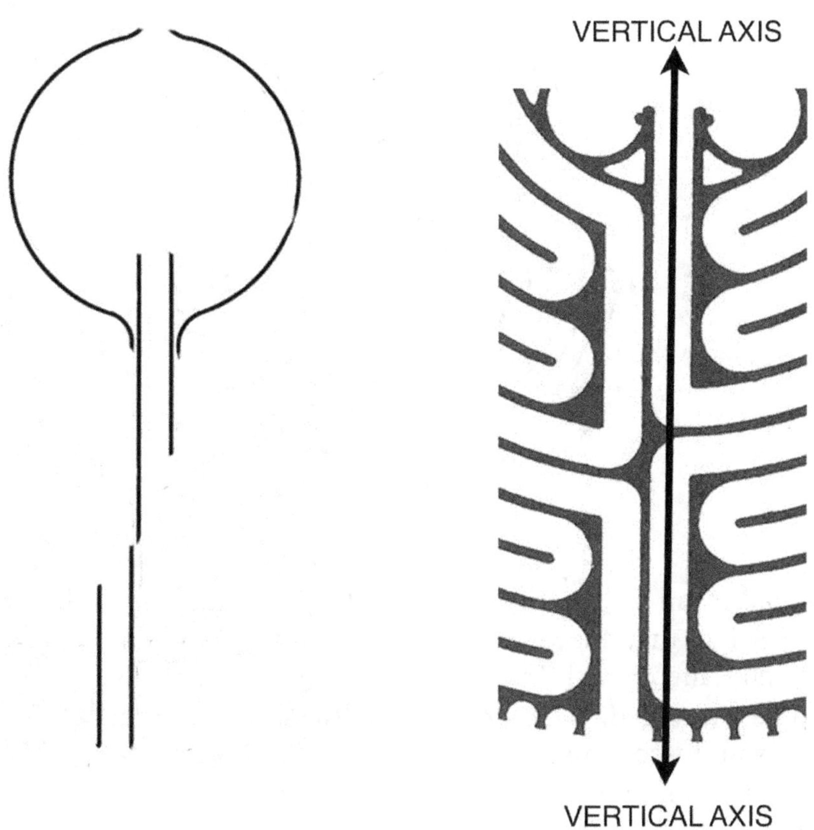

I went on the internet to find an example of a Chartres labyrinth with the axis drawn wrong, coming up with the following drawing with the signs of the zodiac. Look at the labryses (turns) at the top of the labyrinth and then move your eye downward to see that the center entrance line is on the axis. That's not correct.

Note how the entrance into the center is offset to the right. They don't have petals in this drawing, which is a good thing, as they would be very distorted. (I've seen them done that way.)

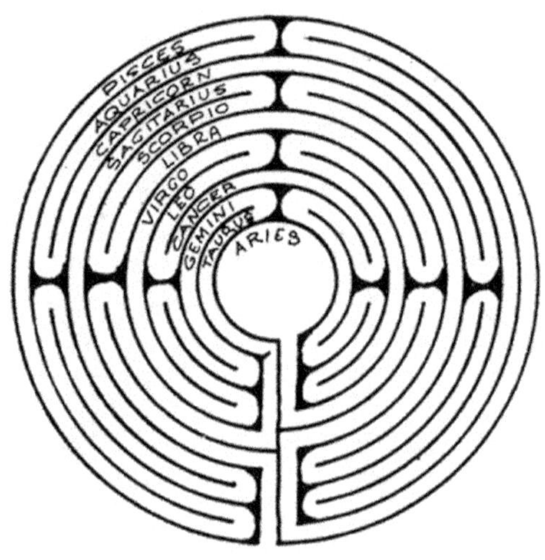

I don't want to get off on too much of a tangent here, but it turns out that there's a story behind this drawing. I have already mentioned the work of Australian architect John James who studied Chartres Cathedral stone by stone for five years and wrote a set of books explaining every aspect of the construction and geometry. I used to hire John to talk to the groups I took to Chartres, and so we became good friends.

The above erroneous drawing is from the website for Studies in Comparative Religion, and more specifically, an article entitled "The Mystery of the Great Labyrinth, Chartres Cathedral" by . . . you guessed it, John James! It's inconceivable that he would draw the labyrinth like that. I suspect the publisher had someone make an illustration. I sent him an email, asking for an explanation. John replied saying he wrote that article forty years ago. He couldn't remember who did the drawing, nor did he seem concerned.

The correct location of the vertical axis is down the center of the righthand entrance path. Stated a different way, the central entrance path is centered on the vertical axis. As a result, the entrance into the labyrinth is to the left of center. Thus I refer to it as the left entrance path, versus the central entrance path (into the center).

As the first turn is subsequently to the left, we call this a left handed labyrinth design. Has there ever been a right handed Chartres pattern? In the Middle Ages, Villard de Honnecourt traveled around and sketched places, some of which we recognize. He was very bad at drawing. His drawing of the western rose window at Chartres is completely wrong. He may have done no better on the labyrinth.

Honnecourt's drawing. Was this supposed to be Chartres or some other labyrinth?

He drew a labyrinth of the Chartres pattern, but without lunations or petals, and right handed. Some historians speculate that it was a different labyrinth, perhaps the one in Sens Cathedral. However, there's no proof of that, and we already have three (different) designs identified as being the Sens labyrinth. With that one exception, I have never seen a right handed Chartres labyrinth, except in Chartres.

What? Well, it was actually the design for the donation box inside the cathedral. The clear plexiglas cover with the labyrinth design was mounted upside down by some unknowing workman, with the result that it was a right handed pattern. I presume it was unintentional. No one seemed to notice.

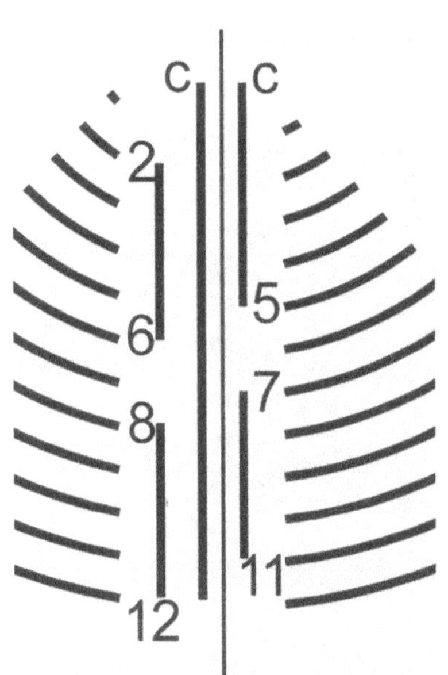

If you are interested in an accurate pattern (canvas, etc.), leave spaces in the two outer entrance lines to allow for the turns that will be there (which I call the detours).

As you see in the diagram (left), circle seven on the left side and circle six on the right side (not numbered in the drawing) will extend to the center line, determining the first turn when entering the labyrinth and the last one before getting to the center. For that reason there's no reason to draw the entrance lines between circles 6 and 8 (left side) and 5 and 7 (right side) as those are walking paths. Now you see why we marked the circle spacing before doing the entrance lines, so we can see where the circles are located and leave the required spaces as described above.

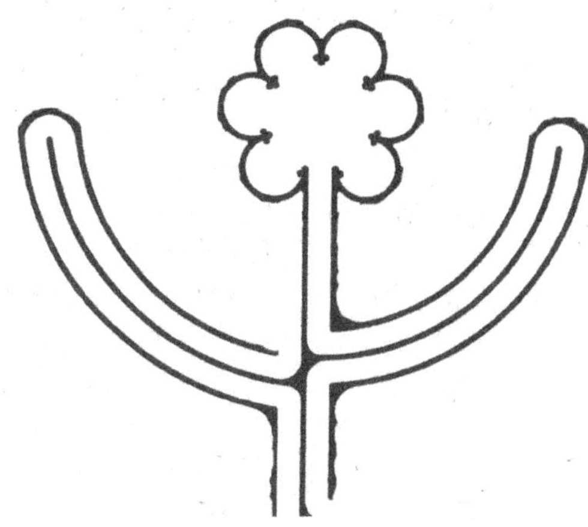

I call the first and the last turns the detours. If you see the center as having petals, the detours can be seen as leaves. To the left I have removed the extraneous lines to show the Chartres flower. I once thought of making this my company logo.

Getting back to business, you can mark the entrance lines in different ways. If you are outside, you can use wire-stemmed engineer's flags, like the ones utility companies use (find them at the hardware store in bundles of one hundred). Or you can put a masking tape dot indicating each line. When I'm drawing (or cutting) the pattern, I put down a strip of masking tape perpendicular to the vertical axis in three places (one near the center, one near the outside, and one in between). On it I make four marks (illustration next page).

The first mark is on the far right, indicating the right side of the central entrance path. That's determined by measuring one-half the path width from the vertical axis. So, if my path is 12" then I would measure 6" to the right and make my mark.

The second mark is half the path width (in this example, 6" again) to the left. I have now established the width of the central entrance path (and hence, all the paths, as they are the same) to be 12".

The third mark is one line width further to the left. This establishes the width of the line, and also marks the right side of the entrance path into the labyrinth.

The fourth mark is one path width further to the left, thus indicating the entrance path.

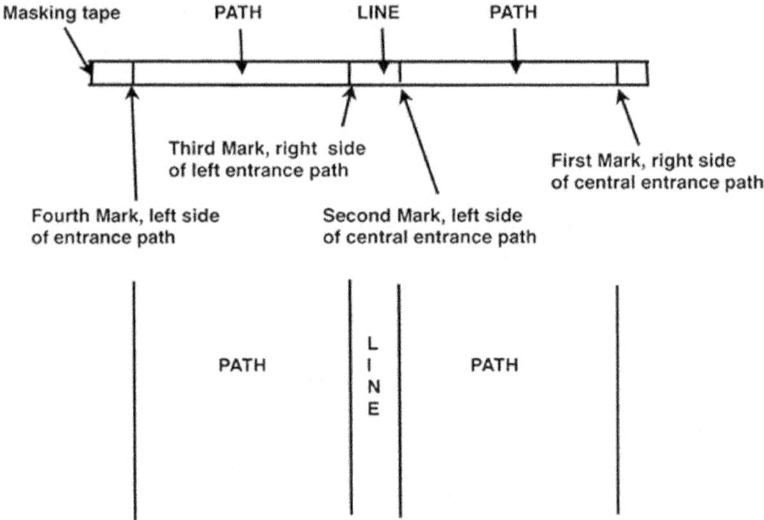

The vertical axis, were it shown, would be up the center of the righthand path.

When drawing the entrance lines on canvas, I use an eighteen-foot-long straightedge. These are the first lines I draw on the canvas. I have found that a soft lead in the mechanical pencil works best (specifically, B2 or B3).

The drawing above shows a typical marking. By doing this three times, I can then use a long straight edge to accurately draw or tape my entrance lines. Outdoors, I may lay stones next to the straightedge to make an accurate line.

You can make a long straightedge by taping together two or more 72-inch straightedges bought at the hardware store. Overlap the ends by a foot or so and tape them together. Alternate them under and over, rather than in a stepped fashion, so they will lay flat.

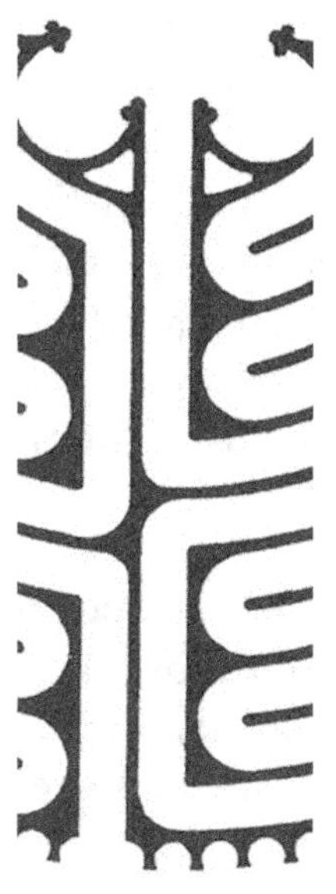

At the end of the two lines that extend into the center (marked "C" on the entrance diagram, p. 66) will be the petal crosses. The tips of those crosses, as we shall see, are at the half-radius point, halfway between the center and circle 1-0. The two central entrance lines, then, extend into the center a few inches short of the half-radius. In our previous example, the diameter of the center was 10' and the radius 5' (60"), so the half-radius point would be at 30". I would stop the entrance lines at about 27" into the center area, to leave room to draw the petal crosses.

Marking the labryses

Before we draw the circles, we want to identify where the turns will be. The back-to-back 180-degree turns are referred to as labryses, in a mistaken association with the mythical two-headed ax.

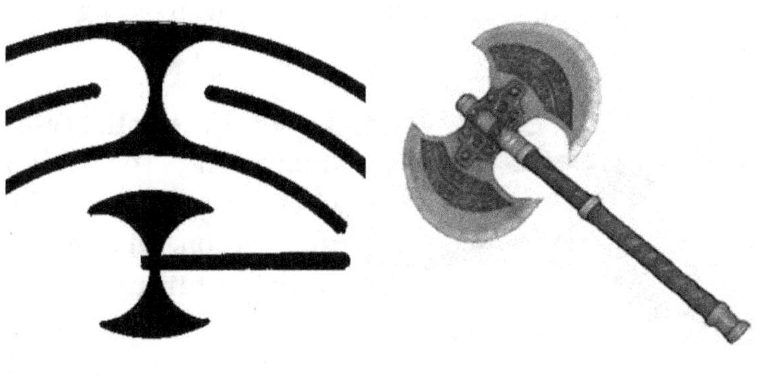

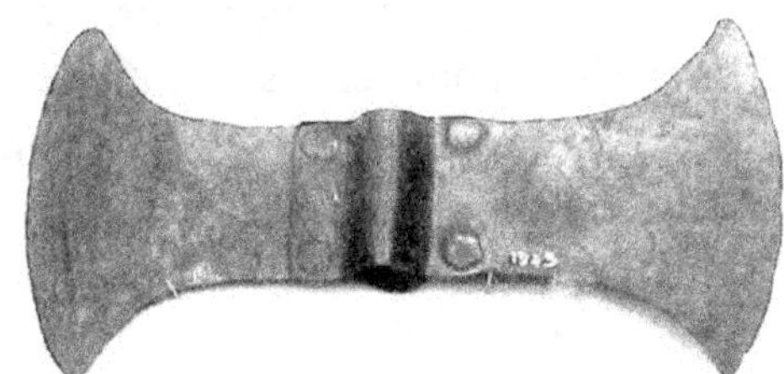

Above left: Turns look somewhat like a labrys
Above: Ceremonial ax
Left: Actual bronze labrys found in a tomb in Masara, Crete.

I agree with scholar Penelope Reed Doub that there's no etymological connection between the words *labrys* and *labyrinth*, even though they share some of the same letters (in different order). Because the labrys was a ritual tool on the island of Crete, perhaps for sacrificing bulls, and the Minoan myth of Theseus and the Minotaur is also from Crete and involves a labyrinth, these two words have been frequently associated. Wrongly, I feel.

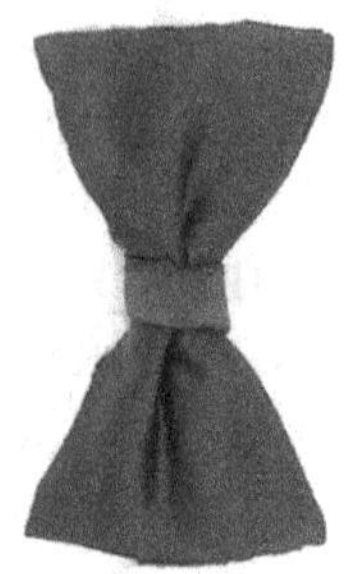

If we are going to make a connection due to shape, why don't we just call them bow ties? Seriously, I agree that labryses and labyrinths both have important mythological symbolism, but not with each other.

To make space for its labrys, each circle stops and then starts up again. I call this breaking the circle. By marking these places, we will avoid drawing the lines out into the path, which would later have to be erased. Even if painting this on the grass, placing a couple of yardsticks in the appropriate place can allow you to skip that little section, thereby avoiding a lot of extra work.

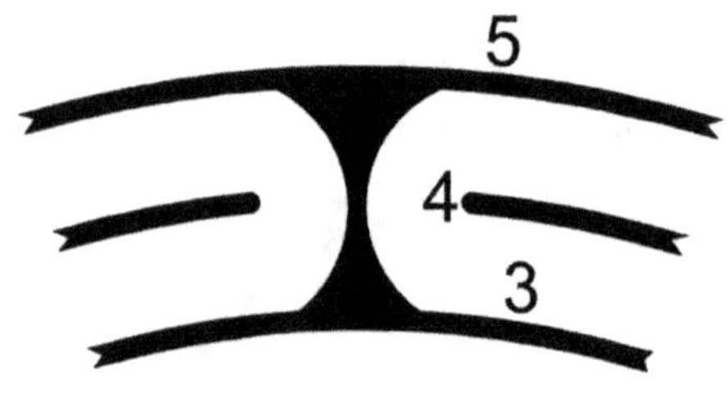

I identify the labryses according to which circle is broken. In the illustration, it's circle four, interrupted to make a turn between the adjacent circuits (paths). There are no labryses on the first or twelfth circles. That leaves ten circles, each of which has one labrys (not counting the half-labryses on either side of the entrance path).

Looking along the top vertical axis, the following circles are broken for turns: 2, 5, 8, and 11; on the right-side horizontal axis, circles 3, 6, and 9; and on the left horizontal axis, the circles 4, 7, and 10. Interestingly, if these turn locations are connected, they form an outward, clockwise spiral (see left).

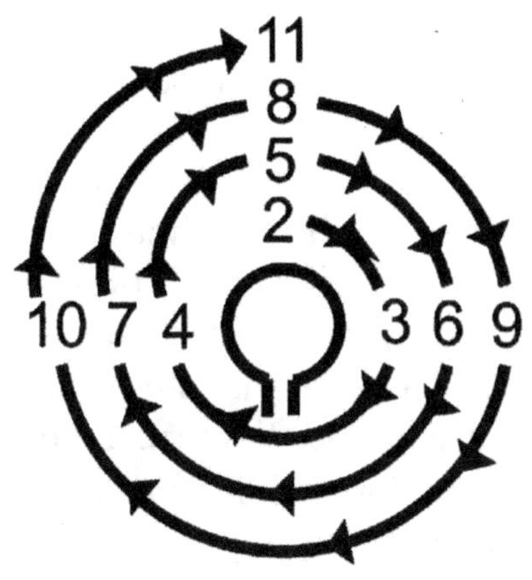

When drawing the circles, we want to leave a space for each labrys by marking a stopping point and starting point. Do this by laying down a couple of yardsticks or strips of masking tape at the point where the circle should stop, and again where it should start up. Along the entrance, the half-labryses can be marked in the same way.

When drawing on canvas, then, we have a line of tape indicating the axis and a series of smaller pieces of tape indicating the interruptions in the circles. Since the position for each of the 12 circles has been indicated on the masking tape axes, it's easy to locate the correct circles and mark the labryses before drawing the circles.

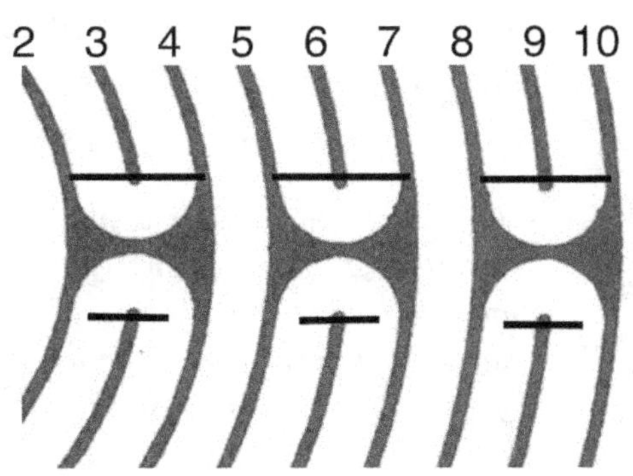

This diagram shows two ways to mark the labryses. It doesn't matter in which direction you may be drawing, as the start/stop indications will be the same. Note that they leave a little room for the half-circle at the end of the line. Shown is the right horizontal axis, in which circle 3, 6, and 9 have breaks for the turns. The lower part of the diagram shows tape just to mark the start/stop of a single line, the one to be broken.

However, if drawing on canvas or scoring into concrete, you can also stop the lines on each side of the broken line for the half-circle (turn). The upper part of the diagram (previous page) shows longer pieces of tape. On the left, there's a start/stop line for 2-o, 3-i, 3-o, and 4-i. That's because 2-o (outer) and 4-i (inner) will become the half-circle of the turn. True, if you continue it as a full line, the extra line will be in a colored area. It may be effectively covered up. But why risk it?

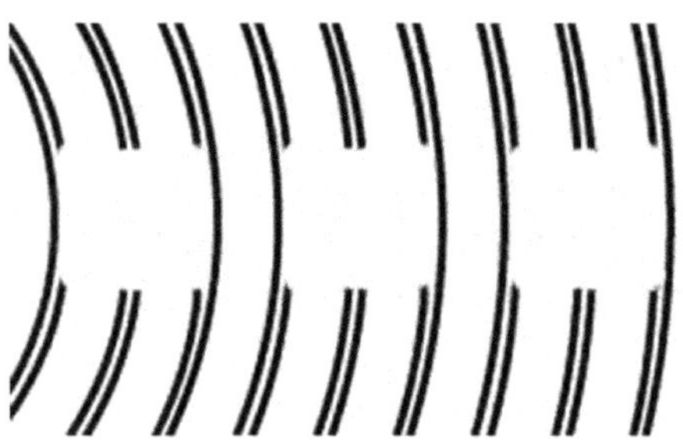

When you have made all of the stops indicated by the masking tape, but have not yet drawn the turns or line ends, your drawing will look like this.

In the pure Chartres pattern, the labrys is slightly wider than the line, whereas in the Veriditas variation, the labrys is the width of the path. In order to properly mark out the labryses you need to know which version you want to make.

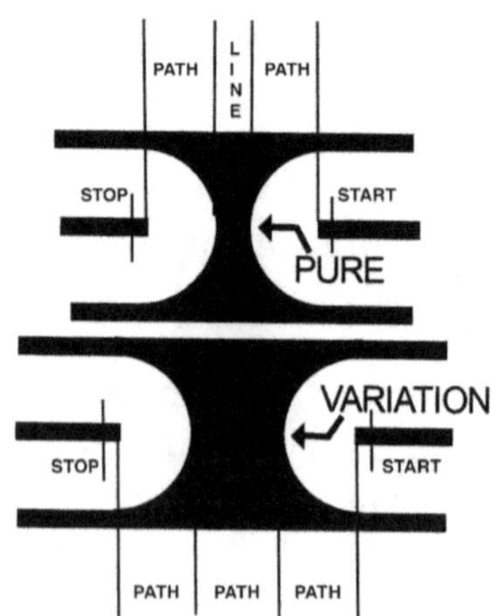

Two labrys configurations, complete with start/stop lines (assuming you draw the circles in a clockwise direction). The top labrys is the width of the line, the bottom the width of the path.

If you are making a masking tape labyrinth, or masking one to paint, there's no need to stop for the labryses. It's easier to just keep going with the circles all the way around. Later, you can just remove a few pieces of tape as necessary.

When we are scoring the pattern into the concrete, we can't make any mistakes, as they can't be erased. In that case, not only do we leave space for the labryses, the space has a particular shape.

If you look at a photo of the Chartres labyrinth, you will see that the half-circles that form the labryses are not aligned. Each one has a slightly different angle. That's because they point toward the center of the labyrinth. As you get closer to the center, the angle gets greater and greater.

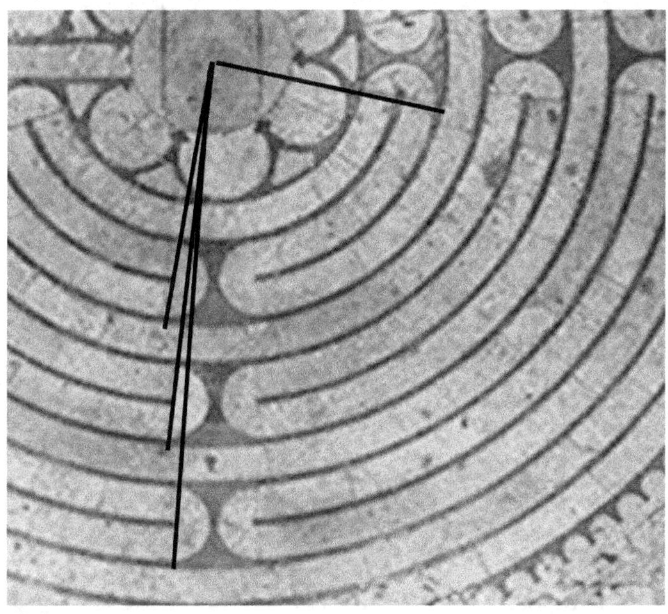

The lines show how the stone half-circles align with the center. We stretch a wire from the center post much like these lines, which indicates exactly where to put the start/stop marks.

There are also half-labryses at each side of the entrance paths. I think it looks funny to use the wide labryses at the turns and use the traditional ones at the entrance, so I make the half-labryses equal to half a path width. That makes sense, full labrys, full path width, half labrys, half path width.

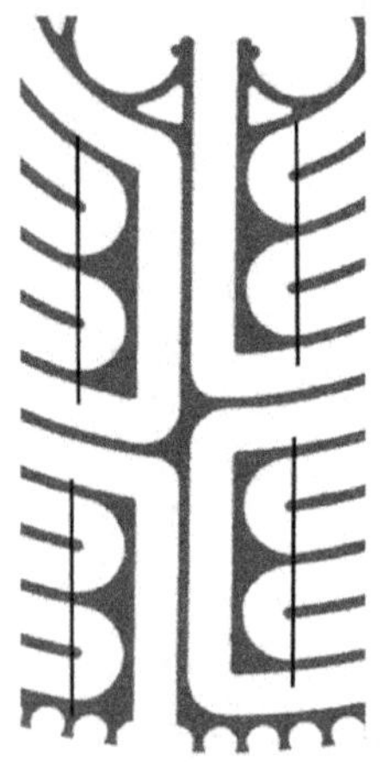

As usual with labryses, at the entrance some lines are stopped for the turns. The other lines can also be stopped because they lead into the half circles. So, essentially, it's easiest to stop all of the lines beside the entrance paths.

The diagram (left) shows four start/stop lines. To be even more accurate, note that these half-turns also point toward the center, as shown for the labryses on page 73. The closer to the center the turn, the more extreme is the angle pointing to the center. Experiment with this when drawing to see my point.

The Center Post

As you can see, there's much preparation before the actual pattern gets drawn. Here is one more item. Before we can draw the circles, we need a center post. There are several possibilities.

<u>Stake in the ground</u>

If the labyrinth is outdoors, you can likely hammer a stake, such as a piece of rebar, into the ground as your center post. Alternatives include a large spike (nails come up to 18" in length), a piece of pipe, or a wooden dowel. It should be sturdy and firmly placed so that it doesn't bend or move.

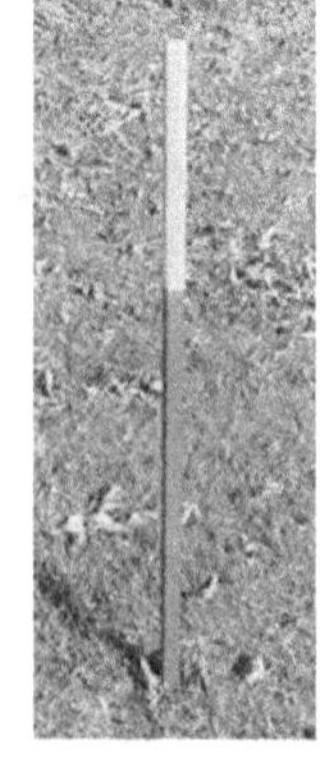

Person

If you are working on a wooden floor, you can take a wooden dowel and put a rubber tip on the end (the kind for folding chairs or canes). Then mark the appropriate spot for the center and have a volunteer hold the dowel firmly in place. This has its drawbacks, especially if the volunteer has a short attention span or gets distracted.

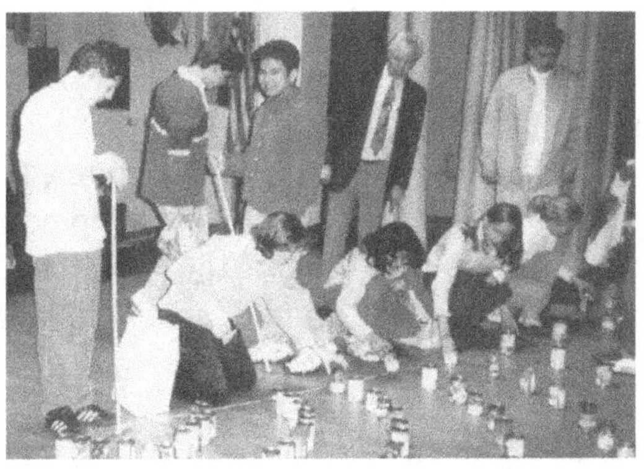

Volunteer holding center post as we make circles with canned goods from food drive.

Weighted pipe and flange

For canvas, concrete, floors and hard surfaces, I use a pipe mounted on a piece of wood, held down by two or three 44-pound Olympic barbell weights. Specifically, I cut a square piece of ¾" plywood around 14" on the side. I draw two diagonal lines from opposite corners to find the center point. Next, I use a 1" paddle drill and make a hole in the center(to be explained momentarily). Or, buy a board made for decoupage, which has finished edges (as in the illustration), find the center and drill the hole.

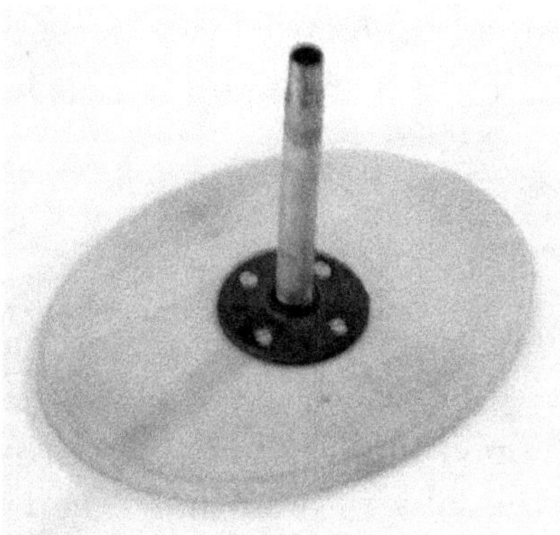

Next, buy a ¾" pipe flange and screw it to the board, centered on the hole. Into the pipe flange you screw a pipe of the desired height (I make mine about 12"). Then you put two or three heavy weights over the pipe, to keep the center from moving. I don't mean little wimpy plastic-covered ten-pounders. I mean serious Olympic weights, with large center holes, that weigh forty-four pounds each. I usually use three.

To mark the center of the labyrinth, lay out the axes, and measure out the path spacing and labrys locations, you need access to the center point of the labyrinth. When those are complete, take the board and put it in the center. Look through the hole to see your center mark and line it up correctly. Then carefully screw in the pipe and add the weights. Or, carefully add one weight, then screw in the post and add the other weights.

You can make a loop at the end of your guide rope and simply put it over the center post. I make mine a bit more complicated. I put a threaded cap on the top of the pipe, into which I drill a hole and fasten a thin threaded bolt, with nuts both inside and outside the cap to hold it in place. Over the thin bolt I put the end of my tape measure.

The end of most tape measures has a little hook so you can catch the end of a board or corner of a wall when measuring it. I use a pliers and straighten out this hook and then, if there isn't one, drill a hole in it. Through this hole I insert a wire loop to go around the center post or put it through the bolt in the top cap.

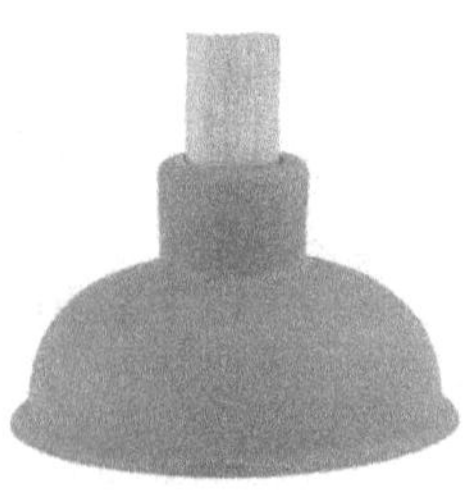

Plunger

Here's one more crazy idea, for making a quick temporary labyrinth. Tape the base of an old-fashioned plunger to the floor in the center of the labyrinth so that it can't move. The loop of the guide rope should fit over the top of the rubber base. If not, include a few inches of the wooden handle.

Whew! Three pages just on the center post. Don't be discouraged by all of these instructions. I'm just trying to be as inclusive as possible for various situations. Plus, I could be a bit obsessed with details.

Drawing the twelve circles

Drawing circles requires some kind of a compass. I have heard tales of some rather amazing contraptions, such as long boards with pegs sticking out. It doesn't have to be that complicated.

If you are outdoors, just use a simple stake for a center post and a guide rope with the circle spacing marked on it. Indoors, you need a different center post, but if you are making a masking tape labyrinth, you can still use a guide rope. For masking tape, do the entrance lines and then make twelve circles. Later you can add the labryses and other details.

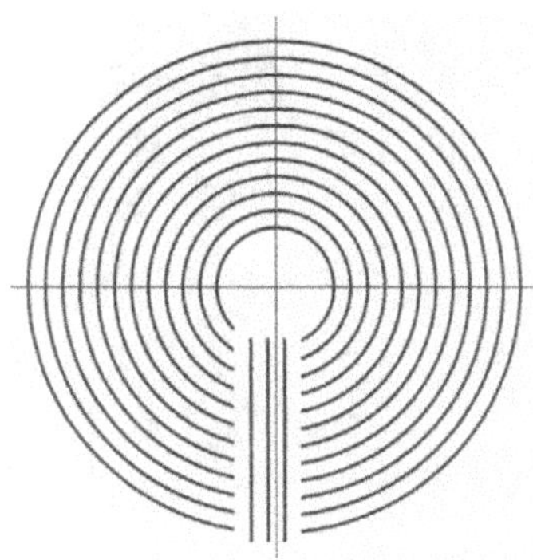

People often call me, befuddled by the prospect of making a temporary labyrinth, and I assure them that once the twelve circles are drawn, everything else will fall in place. Here's what it would look like (left).

A "compass" can be as simple as a stake in the ground with a rope looped around it. However, since rope stretches, I generally use a metal tape measure – not for actually measuring, but because it's very light and easy to handle and doesn't stretch. I attach it to my center pipe as previously explained.

It's possible to make all the circles at one time if you have enough workers. If you are using a tape measure, extend it out past the twelfth circle and engage the lock mechanism that keeps it from rewinding. Then you can use masking tape to mark the circle spacing on the tape measure.

Otherwise, use the guide rope that you have made in advance. You can have one worker for each circle, or one for every two circles. They can be putting down rocks on the ground or, indoors, tiny bits of tape. Then, other volunteers can follow behind and fill in more rocks or connect the dots with lines of tape. Another option is for each person to have a roll of tape. As the leader slowly moves the guide rope, the workers keep taping at their designated mark.

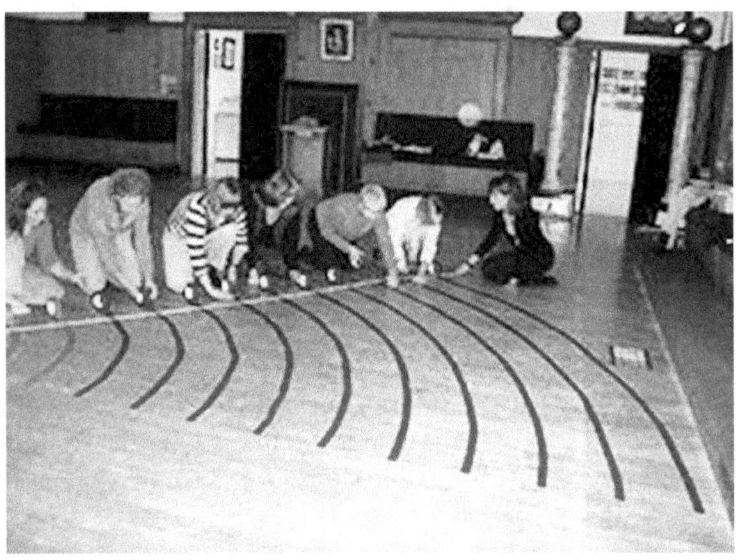

Each person is taping two circles. Photo by Warren Lynn.

On canvas, we use a device that has two pencils, so that we draw both the inner and outer circle at the same time. This involves the use of a yardstick compass. Available at most Dick Blick art stores (about $7.00, see http://www.dickblick.com/products/griffin-yardstick-compass/), this clever device

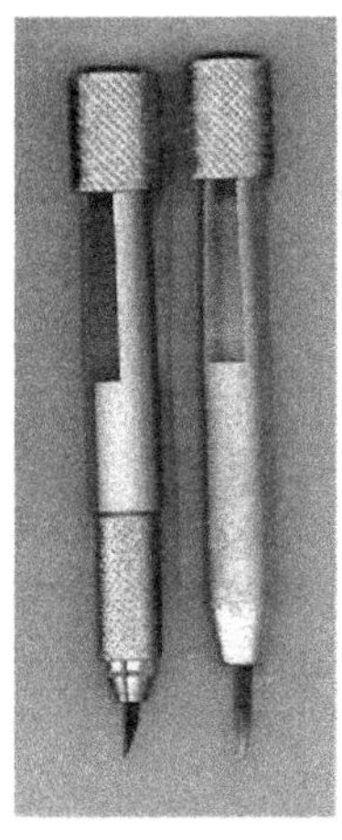

consists of pencil and point with a slot in the middle so they can slide onto a standard size yardstick. By that I mean the "thin" ones. There are also thick yardsticks which won't fit into the slots (such as those from The Home Depot). We will use the yardstick version to make our labryses later on. You can tape two yardsticks together and make a circle eleven feet in diameter. For the circles, we use two yardstick pencils side by side on a piece of yardstick. Clamps attach the piece of yardstick to the tape measure, which is clipped to the yardstick and is attached to the center post (see diagram below).

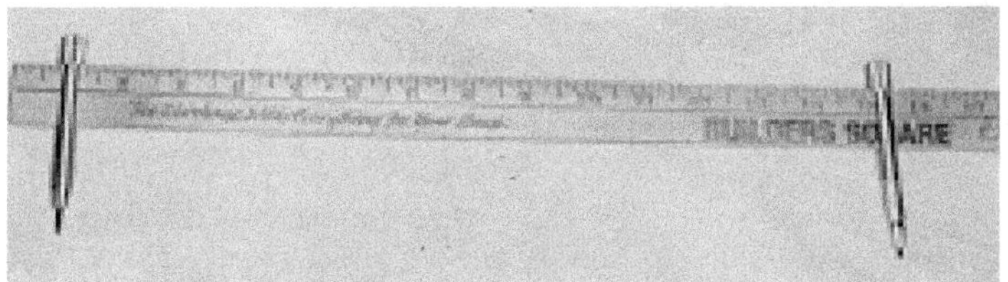

With just a little practice, one can learn to keep a steady outward pressure to keep the tape measure compass fully extended, smoothly and evenly drawing the circles. You can use this tool for drawing on concrete, by taping carpenter pencils or felt markers to the piece of yardstick.

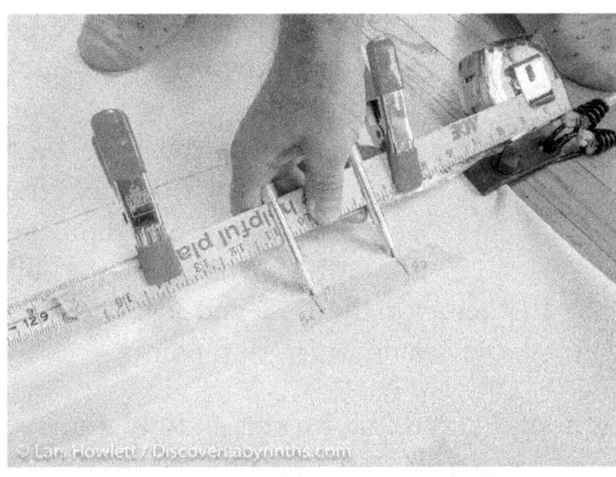

Here, Lars Howlett is lining up the pencils to the marks on the vertical axis. The tape measure is on the other side of the yardstick, held in place by the clamps.

It's necessary to keep canvas from moving, so we use Bungee® cords that clamp onto the canvas on one end (using a tarp clip) and 35-pound dumbells on the other. For our larger labyrinths, such as the Chartres pattern, we used sixteen dumbells. For smaller canvases we use eight.

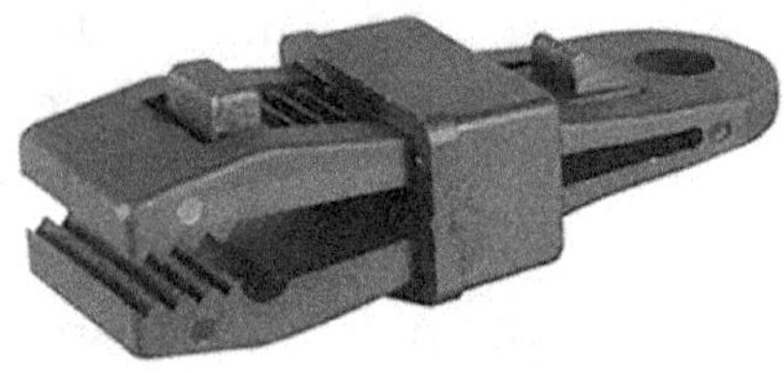

The tarp clip attaches to the edge of the canvas. The hole is perfect for the wire hook of a Bungee® cord. Stretching the canvas keeps it from moving, and, during painting, from shrinking or puckering..

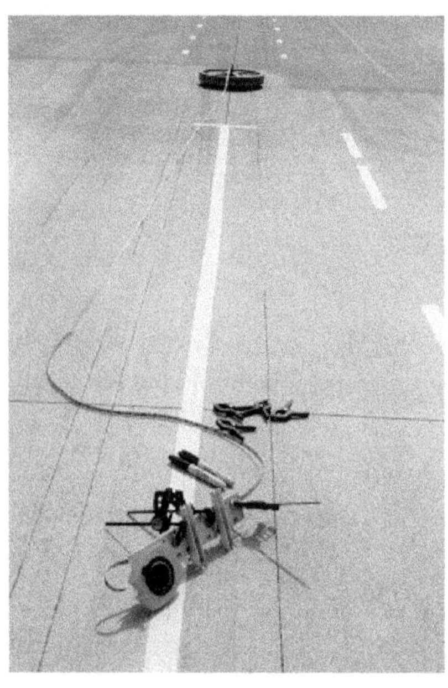

The illustration shows a variation of my usual setup. Since I was drawing on concrete, instead of using pencils I bolted two short pieces of "U" channel to a piece of wood to hold Sharpie® indelible felt-tipped pens (attached with rubber bands).

You can see that I have already drawn the straight entrance lines. The first one was the one on the right, then two for both sides of the center line, and one more on the left. The lines on the left and right have breaks in them for the first and last "detour" turns. The masking tape indicates my start/stop points.

Note: I have never found anything to successfully remove indelible Sharpie® from concrete. It's a bit hair raising trying to get every line exactly right. Each circle starts and stops at both sides of the entrance plus one other place for a turn (except for the first and twelfth circles). Before drawing each circle I verify where I start and stop. Sometimes I have a helper who keeps an eye on me and gives me warning when to stop.

In the center is a pipe mounted on a piece of wood, held down with heavy barbell weights. The end of the tape measure is attached to the top of the pipe, as previously described.

The long row of tape in the foreground marks the vertical axis and contains marks for the circle spacing. (It also covers a control joint in the concrete which was placed on the vertical axis. It can be seen above the weights.) Smaller pieces of tape to the right and at the top indicate where to start and stop drawing the circles.

In the photo on the previous page, the center post, weights, and attachment of the tape measure are the same as I have described in these instructions. It's a system that has served me well. It's very light weight and can be packed for travel.

I usually draw from the outside towards the center. That way, as my legs and back get tired, the circles get smaller and take less time to draw. Judy Hopen, my long time assistant and studio manager, was capable of drawing the circles at a walking speed, bending deeply at the waist to reach the floor. Working together, we once drew an entire Chartres pattern on canvas in four hours. I think that should be listed as a world record.

When drawing the outer circle, if there will be lunations, it's necessary to draw only the inner circle, 12-i, as the outer circle will be the lunations. The reverse is true in the center, drawing only 1-o, as the inner circle will be the petals. For each of these circles, use just one pencil or marker.

With the rest of the circles, place the pencils on each mark, clamp down the tape measure, check everything once more for any small adjustments, and draw the circle. When finished, remove the clamps, line up the pencils on the next mark, clamp them down, and draw again. Repeat for all the circles.

Sometimes we don't draw the circles at all. In one of our technologies, we score the pattern with diamond-bladed tools. That's too technical to cover in this book. In another case, we use a tape machine, which puts down parallel pieces of tape, in the same way that we got two simultaneous lines from dual pencils.

For a saw or taping machine, the compass must have a rigid arm, instead of the tape measure. The taping machine is called a Line Taping Machine (or sometimes a Game Taping Machine, used for laying out gym floor basketball courts). I bought ours from SealMaster (see http://www.sealmaster.net/Tools%20an%20Accessories.shtml).

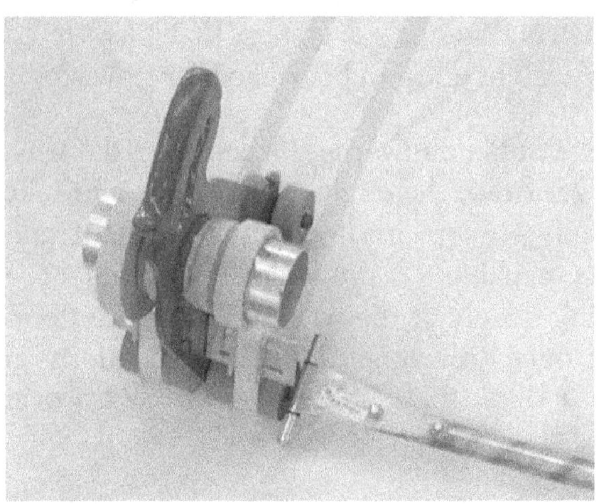

Our line taping machine in action. We have two, one for canvas and one for concrete or floors. It can hold tape up to two-inches wide and lay it down up to four inches apart.

The taping machine makes easy work of laying out the labyrinth circles. Typically, they are done by lunch time. For the smaller details, such as turns, petals, and lunations, we draw them first and then tape along our lines. When taping, be careful to always have the drawn line showing so that it will be covered when the pattern is painted. Otherwise, if we cover up the line, when we remove the tape it will still be visible.

Judy Hopen was such a precise painter that we always drew our canvas labyrinths in pencil, and then she would paint them by hand. For other workers, however, we often used the tape machine and taped the pattern onto the canvas. In such case, it's important to press down on the tape to avoid getting paint under it. I made many experimental devices, but the best one turns out to be the back of a large table spoon.

The company that sells the taping machine also sells a kit with pipes that screw together to make the rigid arm. However, the way the machine connects to the pipes was not suitable for labyrinths. So I had to custom make both a bracket for the tape machine and a multi-directional center (see photo).

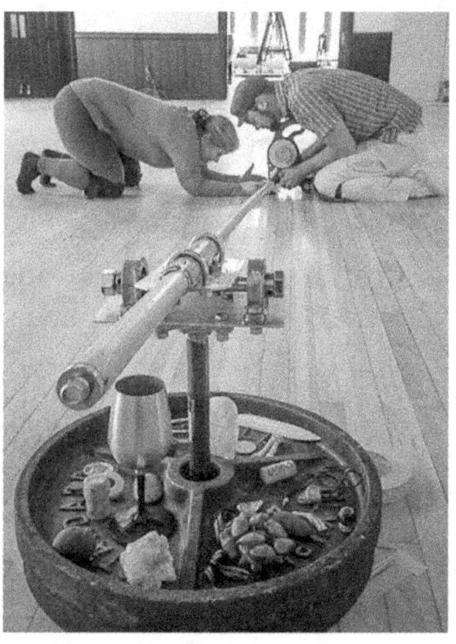

Lars Howlett and Lea Goode-Harris aligning a tape machine to the circle marks to lay out a wooden floor labyrinth.

Again, that's too technical for this manual. If you really need to make such devices, write to me and I'll share my designs. Eventually I hope to write an instruction manual for contractors and professional labyrinth makers that will include such tips. The scope of this book is more modest than that, more for do-it-yourself labyrinths. For general interest, I include the following photos.

Below: Examples of some of our more technical self-designed equipment for scoring patterns into concrete.

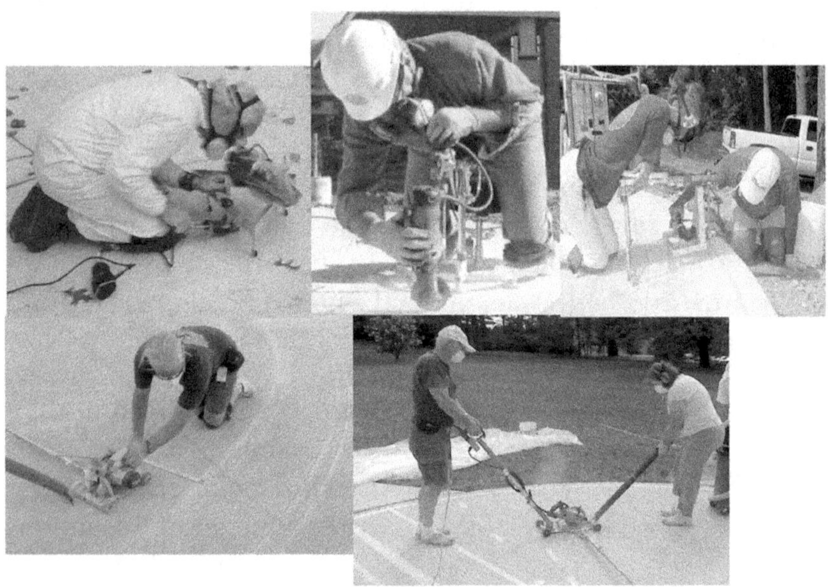

Most likely you will make a labyrinth outdoors by putting down stones on the grass. In such cases, I use a stake for the center post and a guide rope with the circle spacing. Volunteers line up along the rope, while behind them, other volunteers hold five gallon buckets with stones, handing them one at a time to the person along the rope. A third tier of volunteers resupplies the buckets of stones, bringing them from the pile. In this way, you can easily keep fifteen or twenty people involved in the construction.

Start at the entrance, which has been marked out, and make one complete revolution moving the guide rope slowly enough for the volunteers to put the stones in place. Later, others can come back and fill in more stones. The best part is the appearance of the labyrinth. In front of the guide rope is just blank space, and behind it, twelve circles of stones. It's wonderful to behold.

As with masking tape, go ahead and make complete circles (except at the entrance). You can then move stones to make the turns.

Drawing the labryses

We have already marked the location of the labryses in order to leave space for them. This step, drawing the turns, is my favorite part of making the labyrinth, as it converts a bunch of circles into an actual pattern. There's nothing tricky here. Using stones outdoors you can simply eyeball the half-circles that form the labryses.

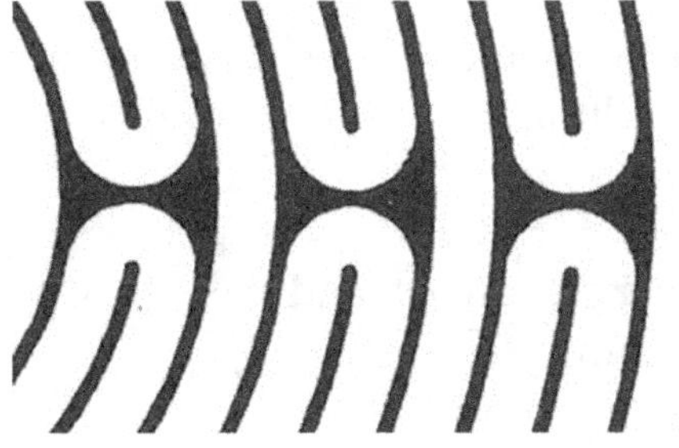

As a reminder, here are the illustrations of labryses. They can be of any width. I have made very large labryses for planting areas within the labyrinth.

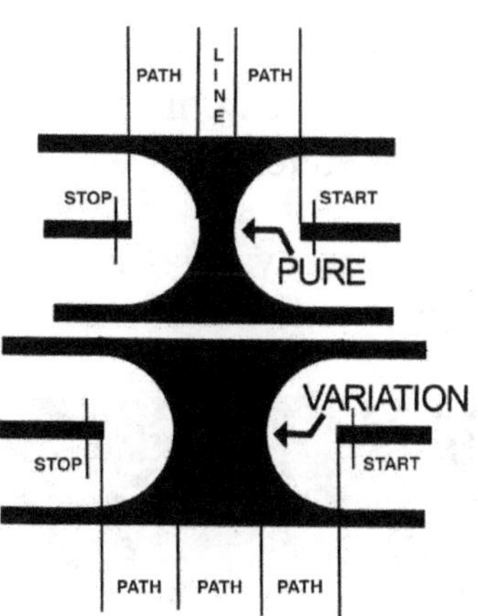

With masking tape, the labryses can just be straight lines, or they can be much more involved. I like to make a rough area filled with strips of tape, and then use an Exacto® knife taped to a yardstick to trim a smooth circle. Removing the excess tape then gives a lovely looking labrys which adds to the beauty of the labyrinth, especially for something likely to be so temporary.

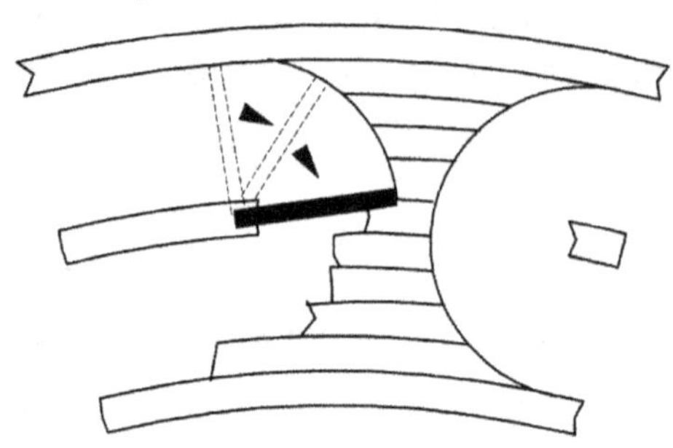

Trimming the masking tape labrys with a yardstick and Exacto® knife.

Draw the turns using a yardstick compass, as pictured earlier. To make an adjustable compass, I use two pieces of yardstick, one with the point and the other with the pencil. With clamps or masking tape, I connect the two pieces at the correct length (the desired radius). The same tool can also be used for the petal circles in the center. For the lunation circles, however, we will use a template.

I find the yardstick compass very compact and easy to use. However, you can use a regular compass.

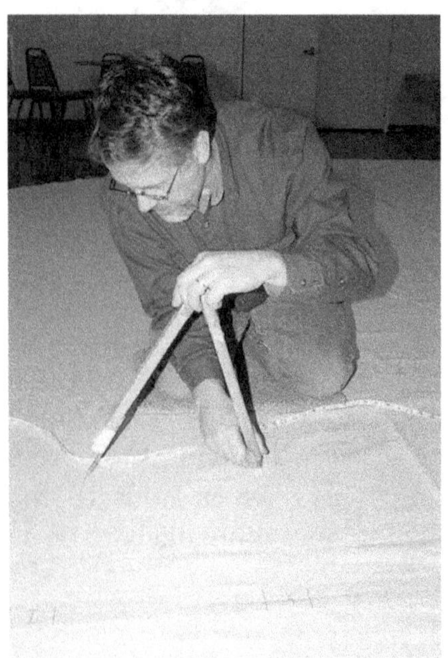

Here, John Ridder is drawing a labrys on canvas. Note in the foreground there's a strip of tape with his circle markings on it. He prefers a cloth (or fiberglass) measuring tape rather than a metal tape measure. (Photo by Warren Lynn.)

So at this point, we have made the entrance, circles and labryses. By looking at a diagram, you can figure out how to do the entrance turns, which are half-labryses. Notice that the left and right sides of the entrance are identical, except turned 180 degrees to each other.

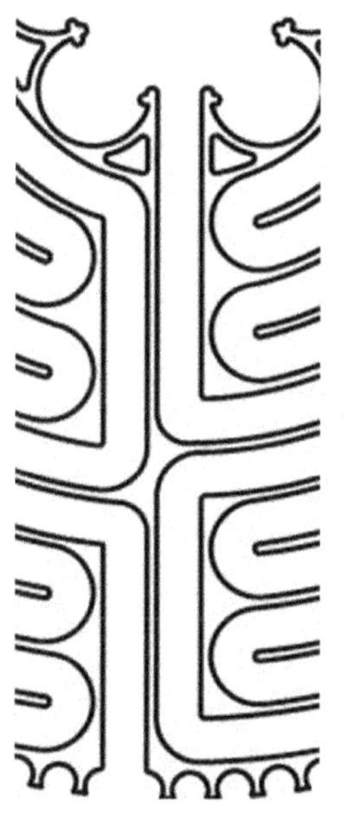

The entrance has two pairs of turns on each side, taking up eight of the eleven circuits. That leaves three more to account for. The detour turns use two adjacent circuits, leaving only one more pathway.

The entrance into the labyrinth goes past the lower pair of turns and goes left. It makes a detour and returns to go around the upper pair of turns. So, on that side, the final circuit is at the inside, next to the center circle.

Exiting from the center, the same relationship pertains: go past one pair of turns, detour, then go around the other pair of turns.

The Line ends

On canvas, draw half-circles for the line ends. Make a template from file folders or poster board if they are to be used for one project. I make mine out of thin polycarbonate, a durable and flexible kind of plastic. The template needs to be slightly smaller than the line width, as the pencil (or felt marker) line will be outside of the template. If the lines are 3" then make the line end template 2 7/8" or even 2 3/4".

The line end half circle connects the inner and outer line of each broken circle. If the template isn't quite the right size, you can fudge by drawing part of the half-circle and then moving the template so that the second part comes out exactly right.

Outdoors, with rocks, we sometimes put a larger stone at the end of each line, to anchor it.

So, we've come quite a ways in drawing the Chartres labyrinth.

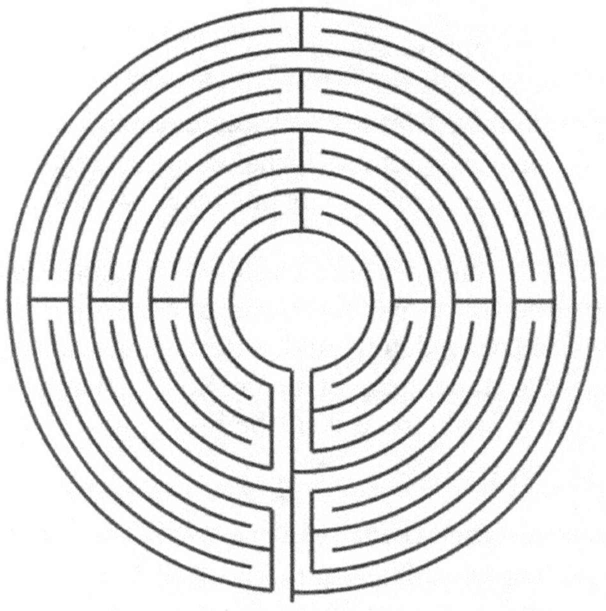

Circles, entrance lines, and turns completed.

It looks a little barren, don't you think? This much of the pattern was known several hundred years before Chartres Cathedral was built. What distinguishes the Chartres labyrinth are the unique petals and lunations, which are not found on any other pattern (except for modern variations). Let's get on to the next steps.

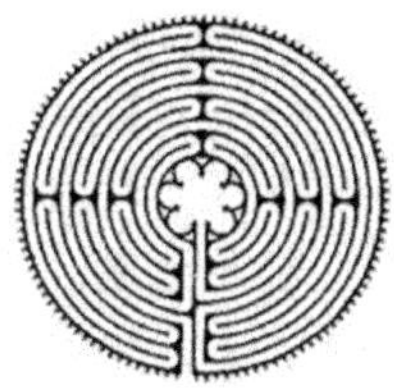

The Petals

Previously we learned the secret of the petals, that they are based on a geometric figure of seven circles, the number seven known as "the virgin."

We know that the tips of the petal crosses are halfway between the center of the labyrinth and the outside edge of the first circle. In Chartres Cathedral, there was once a plaque in the middle of the labyrinth (portraying Theseus and the Minotaur), now long since removed. It would have emphasized the size of this half-radius circle, touched by the petal tips.

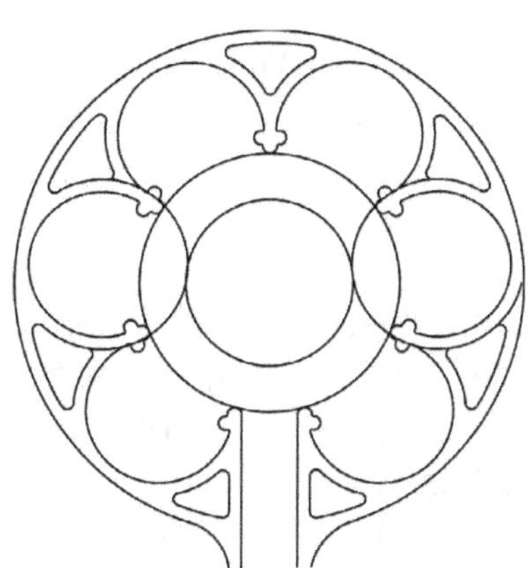

We also know that the outer petal circles are one-third the diameter of the center. In this diagram you can see how the outer petal circles overlap, thus consolidating the petals enough to allow for the entrance path. Understanding the nature of these two center circles is very helpful in understanding the pattern.

The key to drawing the petal circles is to first locate and draw the petal crosses. We can locate the top petal cross as it's on the vertical axis. We can also find the half-crosses on either side of the entrance path. (Note that these crosses have only one arm, so that they don't stick out into the entrance path.)

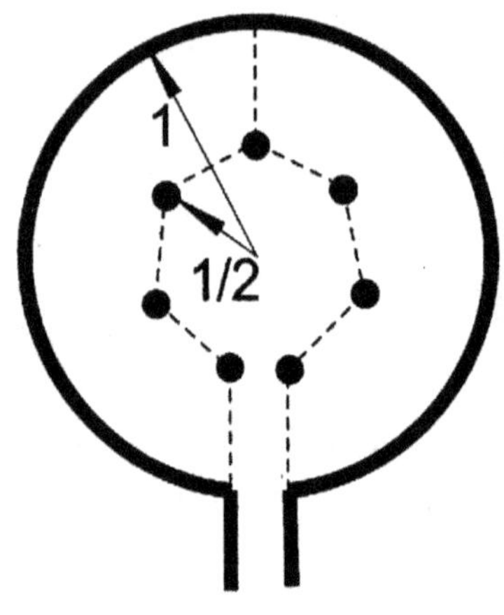

That leaves only four more petal crosses to be located, two on either side. This can be done through a simple process of estimation and correction. Since you can be accurate about the mid-radius point, in estimating the location of these crosses you will only be guessing at the spacing between them. Visually, you can place an object or a piece of tape where you think the points should be located. Just make your best guess.

Let's say the radius of the center circle is 60". That means the half-radius is 30". By using two yardsticks, you can measure out from the center 30" with one, and measure the space between the tips of the crosses with the other.

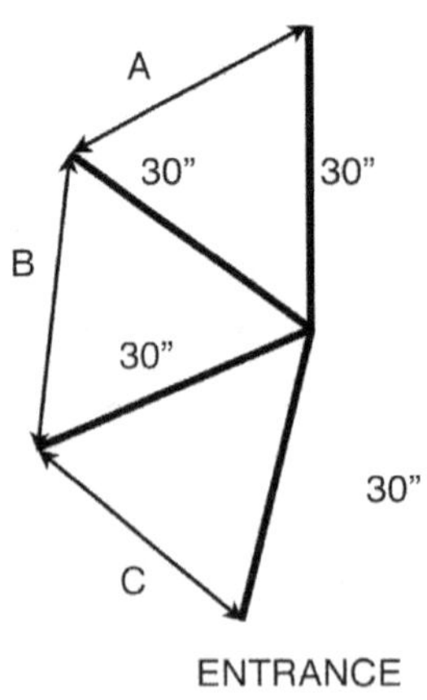

On the left is a diagram of the left side of the center circle. Using the above example, the half-radius is 30". Since the half-radius marks are consistent (in this case, 30") the variation comes from the space between the petal crosses, here shown as A, B, and C.

Measure the length of A, B, and C, add them up and divide by three. This average should be the correct distance for them to be spaced apart.

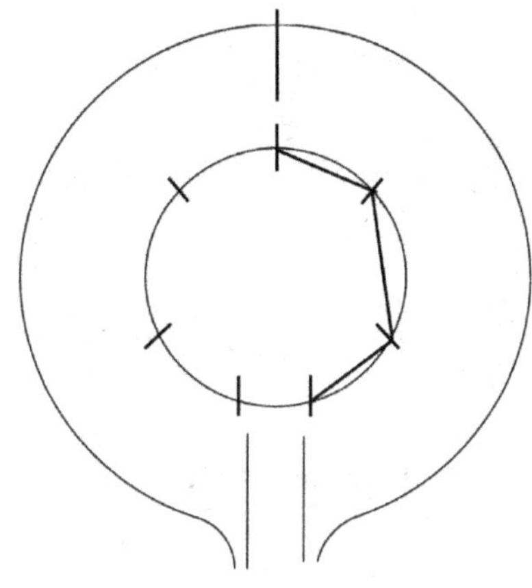

Here's another view. All possible points 30" from the center would comprise a circle. Here, rather than lines as in the previous diagram, I drew a circle to demonstrate that aspect of the relationship (half-radius). You don't have to draw a circle there. It's for demonstration purposes only to show that all petal tip marks will lie that distance from the center.

Three of the marks we can easily locate. The top one is on the vertical axis. The other two are at the entrance. You will note that the marks I have made don't line up with the entrance lines. This is because we are marking the center of the petal cross (see diagram, right).

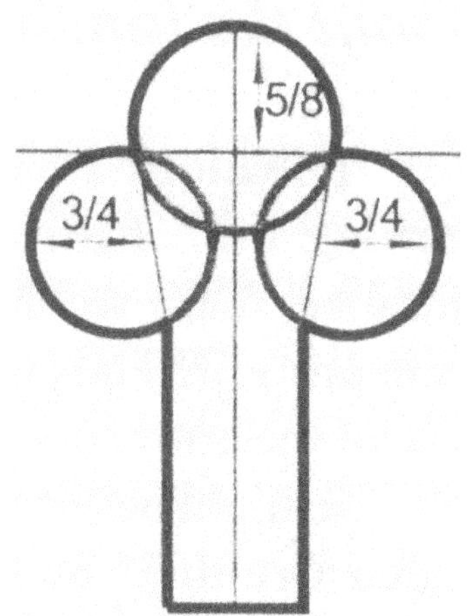

The petal crosses are not a standard cross with rounded arms, although I see this done frequently.

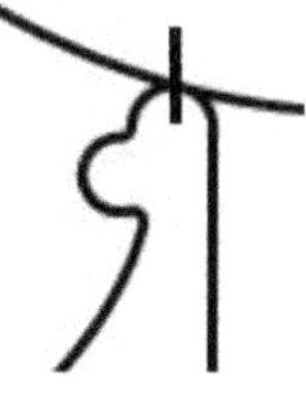

The lower part of the template (left) represents the width of the line. The petal cross is located where two petal circles come together. The bottom of the cross indicates their closest point, which is the width of the line. As the petal circles keep going, the space between them increases. The top circle of the cross represents how far apart the petal circles would be at that point. Hence, the top circle is larger than the line width and the side circles.

How large are the side circles? They are an average of the top circle and the path width. Suppose the line width is 3", as it is in Chartres. The top circle of the petal cross has a diameter of 3½". The side circle, then, lies between those two values, namely, 3¼".

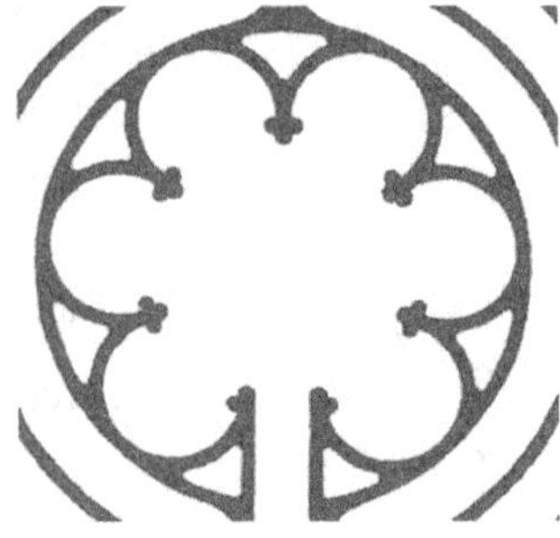

How the three circles within the petal relate to each other is shown by the fraction of the diameter by which they extend outward (see previous diagram). This is very counter-intuitive at first, until you draw it with CAD on the computer (left). Then it becomes clear that a certain logic prevails.

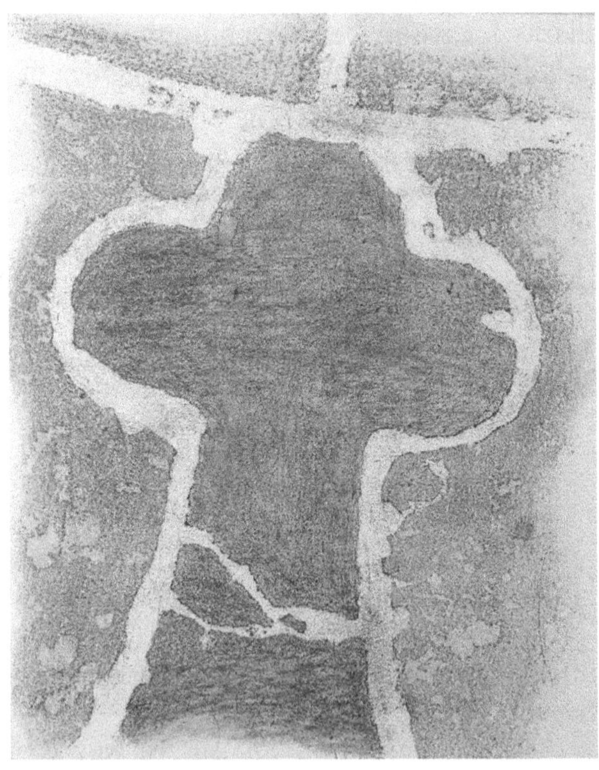

I arrived at these conclusions about the petal crosses by making tracings of the actual ones in Chartres and then drawing on them. Here is an actual rubbing. Feel free to copy and enlarge it to study or even to use as a template.

I now make my templates out of polycarbonate, but I used to make them from galvanized sheet metal. Here are the templates that I once used to draw many labyrinths.

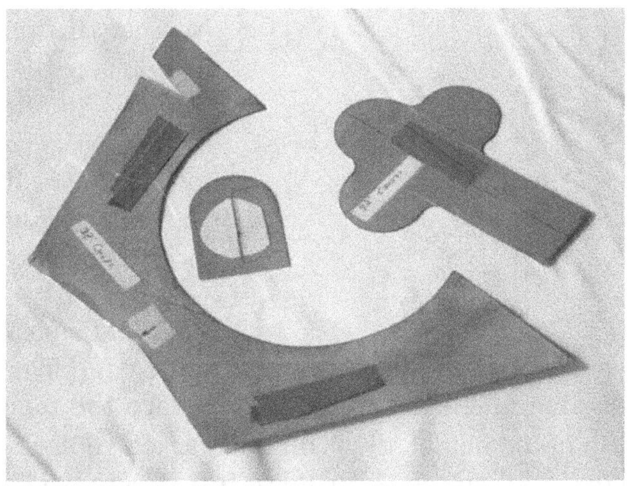

The largest template is for the lunations, which we shall address shortly. The smallest is for the line ends. The petal cross contains a masking tape "handle" for picking it up and moving it, and a line down the center axis for alignment.

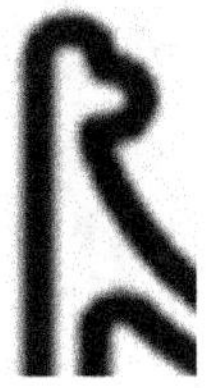

When drawing the entrance petal crosses, the top circle of the cross aligns with the entrance line (see left). That point is hard to see on an opaque template, such as sheet metal, as the arm of the cross gets in the way, but easy to see when the template is made of clear plastic.

Now lets get back to those petal cross marks. Here again is the diagram that shows the three known marks (top, entrance) plus two more marks on each side. The right side of the illustration shows three lines connecting the petal marks. Note that they aren't all the same length. That's because I just guessed where they were located, just as you will.

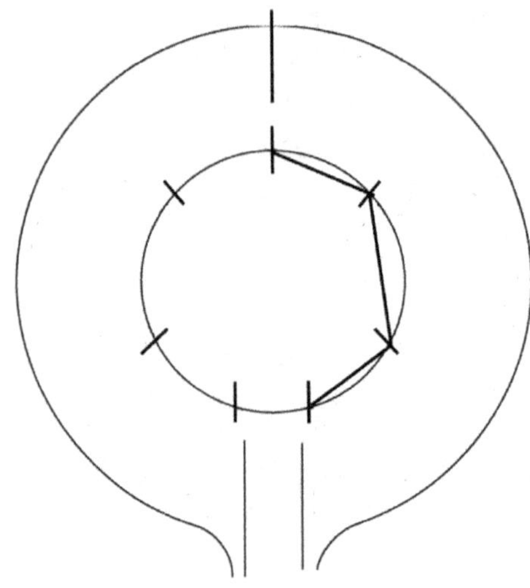

Suppose your three measurements are 23 inches, 21 inches, and 25 inches. Add these together and divide by three, yielding the average (in this case, 23). That's the correct spacing for the petal crosses. Now you know how to locate them, on the half-radius point and 23 inches apart.

When drawing the petal crosses, make sure they point toward the center. That's what the center line on the template is for. Place the template so that the tip of the petal cross is on the marked spot. Then use a straightedge to align the template so that it points towards the center of the labyrinth (using the center line for that purpose).

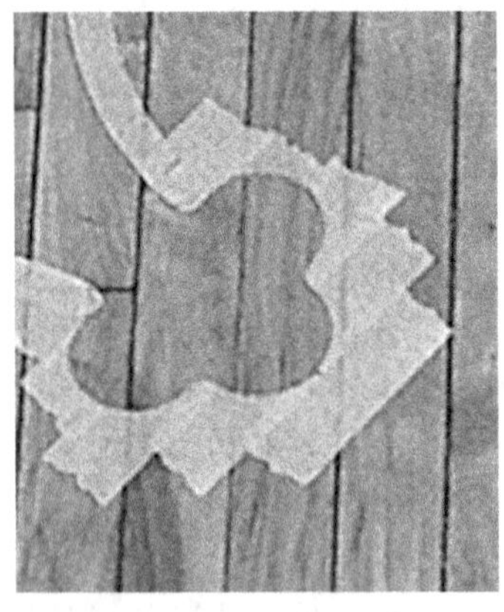

When the template is properly in place, use a pencil (canvas) or marker (concrete) to trace the petal cross. But wait, here's one more time saving suggestion. Before drawing the cross, put down pieces of masking tape to form an area larger than the cross. Then, draw the cross on the masking tape, aligning it as previously described. Finally, use an Exacto® knife and cut along the line, removing the inside portion. The example to the left was made by Lars Howlett and Lea Goode-Harris for a labyrinth in Ross, California.

The previous discussion related to accurately drawing the petals. When making the labyrinth with tape or rock you won't need a template. However, you can use the same layout system. Place a rock at the petal cross locations, then make the petal circles.

The Petal Circles

Once the crosses are in the right place, success with the petals is assured. You simply use your yardstick compass to connect the petals. Before you proceed, decide which version of the Chartres pattern you are making, the pure or the variation.

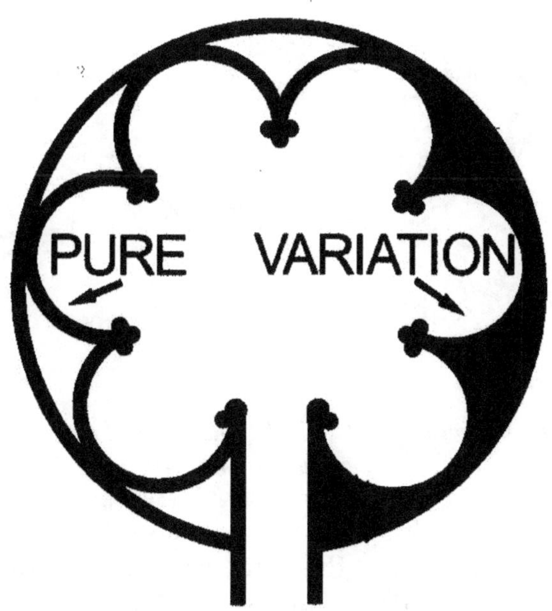

If you used the wider labryses, as described earlier, you may want to balance that additional colored area by filling in the space between the petal circles. With the traditional, pure Chartres design, an inner and outer circle comprise the petals, whereas for the variation, only the inner circle is needed. The variation is easier to draw, but takes more paint.

If drawing a pure Chartres pattern, you can use two pencils as you did with the large circles, or draw the circles separately. You align the pencils to three points. On each end of the petal circle you connect to the petal crosses that have already been drawn. The third point is at the first circle.

If you are drawing with two pencils, then you simply line them up with the outer first circle (1-o). If you are drawing the variation, however, the inner petal circle must allow for the width of the first circle, for which there's no line. That means you must measure the line width and make a mark for you to use when drawing the petal circle (shown by the "X" in the diagram below).

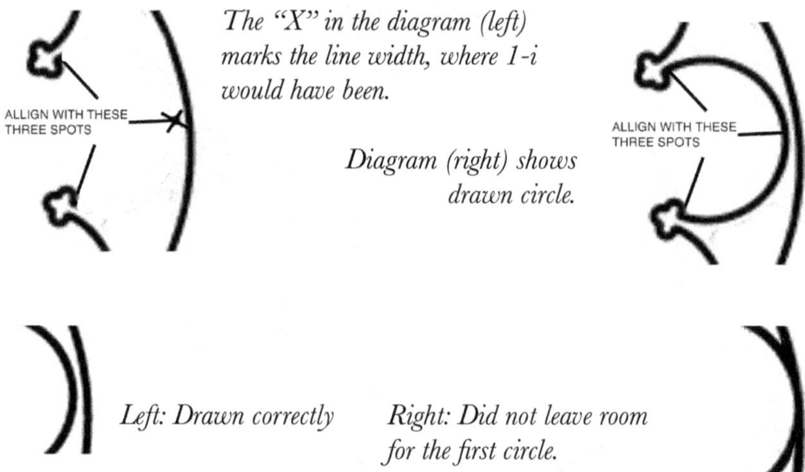

The "X" in the diagram (left) marks the line width, where 1-i would have been.

Diagram (right) shows drawn circle.

Left: Drawn correctly

Right: Did not leave room for the first circle.

The above diagram shows the petal circle drawn correctly and incorrectly. I have seen a number of labyrinths drawn the "wrong" way, which is why I am showing this distinction.

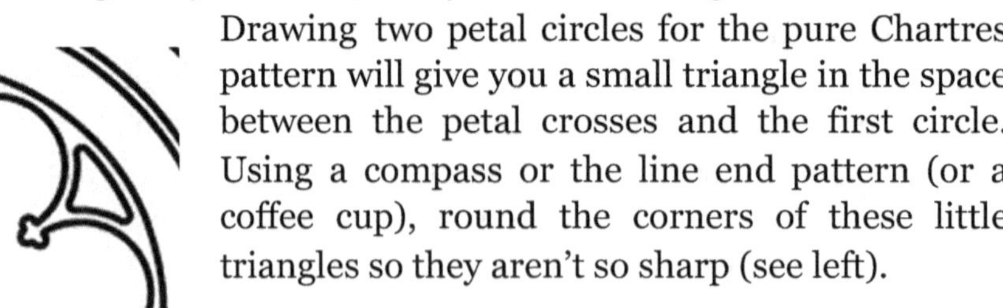

Drawing two petal circles for the pure Chartres pattern will give you a small triangle in the space between the petal crosses and the first circle. Using a compass or the line end pattern (or a coffee cup), round the corners of these little triangles so they aren't so sharp (see left).

As you draw the petal circles, you will find what seems to be a discrepancy. The two circles beside the entrance are larger than the other petal circles. Don't worry, that's normal. It's caused by the fact that the entrance crosses don't point toward the center.

I have found that I have two choices. If I make the petal circles all the same size, then the petal crosses won't be equidistant. Vice versa, if I make the petal crosses equidistant, as we have, the circles won't be the same size. Visually, I feel that is the best choice.

One day while in Chartres I decided to measure the labyrinth to see which solution the mason chose. The answer? Both! The circles were the same size and the petal crosses equidistant. This is made possible by the presence of mortar, that allows for some fudging. I have accomplished the same feat in CAD, but it's very difficult. So I prefer to use the method I am teaching here.

While the petals and lunations aren't required for a labyrinth, I think they add a lot to the appearance, energy, and feel of the labyrinth, making it worthwhile to take the extra time to draw them. So, let's take a look at the lunations.

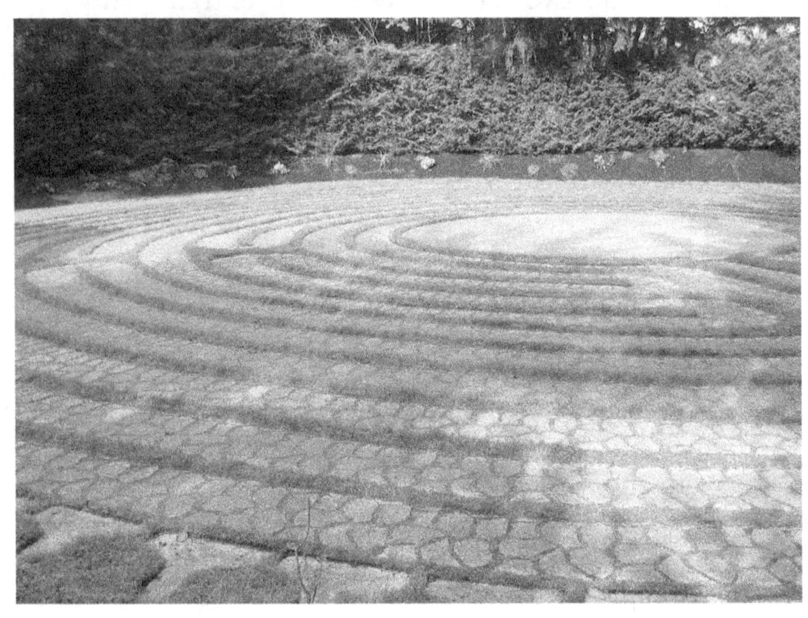

Chartres labyrinth at Bethlehem Retreat Center, Nanaimo, British Columbia, Canada

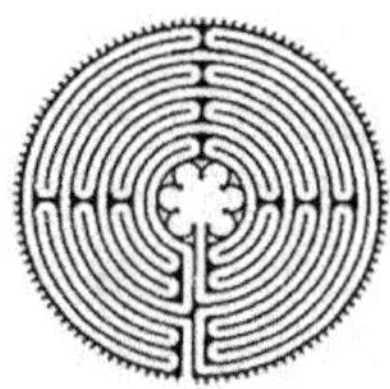

The Lunations

The lunations are often a source of consternation. Once you have a few hints as to their arrangement, they become much more manageable.

Here are some numbers: Were there no entrance, there would be 114 lunations. With one missing for the entrance, there are 113. Thus there are 113 teeth. Since there's a partial circle at each side of the entrance, there are only 112 complete lunation circles, plus the two half circles at the entrance.

Lunations is not the universal word for these arcs. They are also called cogs or teeth. I like *lunations* because 112 represents four lunar months of twenty-eight days. The lunar calendar determines the date for Easter. Moreover, lunar symbolism denotes the Virgin Mary (solar, Jesus).

It might be tempting to simply draw the lunations using CAD (Computer Aided Drafting) by dividing the circumference by 114. Unfortunately, the result is not consistent with the original design for the following reason. In Chartres, there's a tooth directly centered at the top of the labyrinth on the vertical axis. If you divide by 114, the tooth will be off-center, to the right. That's always a hint on how the drawing was done. If the top tooth is off center, the lunations are equally spaced.

Scarlet, the designer of the labyrinth, wanted a tooth on the vertical axis. So he moved the top tooth to the left. As a result, the lunations on the left side are slightly more squeezed together (smaller), and on the right side, slightly larger. That's why calculations that make them all equal don't work out. The tiny difference, multiplied by fifty-some lunations on each side, can result in a considerable error (five or six inches).

In Tennessee, I visited a beautiful terrazzo labyrinth made with great skill by a local company. But they didn't know the secret of the geometry of the lunations. They calculated their size on CAD, assuming they were all the same. In terrazzo construction, metal dividers are attached to the concrete to separate the different colors. For a labyrinth in Oregon, I once drew the pattern onto a concrete pad in Sharpie® marker. The terrazzo company then installed the dividers on my lines.

For the labyrinth in Tennessee, they started at the top of the labyrinth, fastening down the lunation circles. Only when they reached the entrance did they realize their mistake. By then it was too late. As a result, it looks like the illustration. Oops.

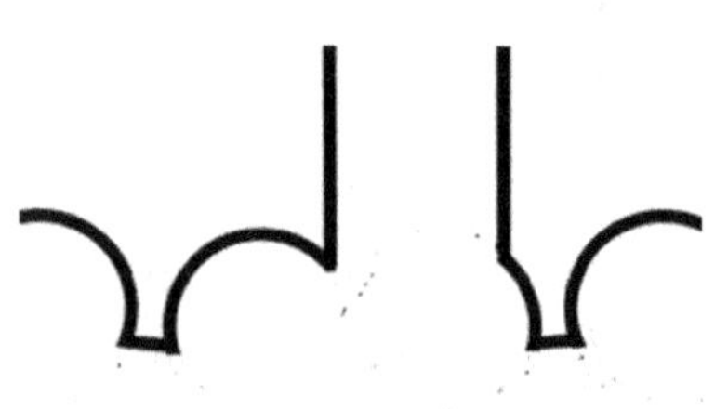

I always use that example as an argument to hire a professional labyrinth maker to assure the geometry is correct.

If you insist on using a computer, start with one tooth at the top followed by 55 teeth on the left side of the labyrinth and 57 on the right side, for a total of 113. If marking the circles, there are 57½ on the left and 57½ on the right.

I frequently read that there are 28½ lunations in each quadrant of the Chartres labyrinth. In fact, none of the quadrants has that number. They vary from 26 (lower left) to 29 (lower right). This irregularity is cause by the entrance being in the lower left quadrant.

To determine the accuracy of the stone carvers who made the original labyrinth in Chartres Cathedral, I measured the six places in which there are four lunations carved into a single piece of stone. That means there are no joints or mortar between them. The first measurement was 52¼”. The next four measurements did not vary by more than $^{1}/_{16}$th of an inch, across a distance of almost four and one-half feet in limestone four inches thick! That’s astounding.

The sixth one, however, was off by two inches. Huh? Hey, masons are human, too. They came around to the end (perhaps having never previously made a labyrinth) and said, “Oh, shoot, we have two extra inches,” so they fudged mightily. If you know where to look, those lunations are noticeably larger than their neighbors.

Fudging, it seems, is a time-honored practice that’s very useful in making labyrinths. That’s exactly what we will do when we use our template to draw the lunations.

Laying out the lunations

When laying out marks on the inner 12th circle for the lunations, I find it easier to indicate the location of the circles rather than the teeth. While the spacing of the lunations equals the width of the path, that measurement extends between the center points of the lunation circles. When marking the location on the twelfth circle, the spacing is slightly less than the path width.

For example, if the path width is 12”, I would first estimate the lunations on the left side to be around 11⅝”. On the right side, I would estimate 11¾”.

We start at the entrance to mark out the lunations, but first, we must go to the top of the labyrinth and mark out two spots on either side of the vertical axis, each of them one-half the distance of our lunation spacing. These mark the circles that will determine the top tooth, and give a target mark when laying out the rest of the lunations. By marking them in advance, we can be sure that the top tooth is right in the center.

Start to the right of the entrance path, using a piece of yardstick with the estimated spacing marked on it. Measure from the entrance line along the inner twelfth circle one full spacing unit. That's mark number one. Then make mark number two and the rest of the marks. Put the mark outside of the circle 12-i, so that it will be in the painted area. (If it were on the inside of 12-i it would be in the pathway, and would be seen.)

Continue in your counterclockwise direction until you have the correct number of marks (fifty-seven). Then see where you are in relation to your target mark. If you are blessed by the stars, you may come out exactly right, which I have done once or twice. Normally, the spacing will be a little off. Your final mark will either be a little short, in which case your circles were a bit too small, or you will overshoot the mark, in which case the circles were a tiny bit too large.

If you miss the mark by a huge amount, something is wrong. Count your marks again and check your measurement. The discrepancy shouldn't be more than a few inches. If you were 1/8" off, then after fifty-seven marks you would be 7 1/8" off. If your discrepancy is half of that, say, around 3", then the correction needs to be about 1/16".

If you come within an inch or so of the target mark at the top, that's close enough. We will learn how to make the adjustment when drawing the lunations. More discrepancy than that will require redoing some of your marks. Let's say you were a little short of the target and have now adjusted your measurement to make the circle 1/16" larger. Don't go back to the entrance. Instead, start at your target mark and work backwards.

As you go, cancel out your previous mark. You will see the space between the first set of marks and the new set get smaller and smaller. At some point, you will find that the new and old marks coincide. Stop there. You have successfully marked out the lunation spacing. The slight difference in the two sets of marks (the second set, and the remaining first marks) will cause no problem when drawing the lunations.

Repeat the same measuring process for the left side of the labyrinth, laying out marks in a clockwise direction, starting at the entrance. This is the side that is slightly smaller, so reduce your measurement for the right side by 1/8". On this side there should be fifty-five marks.

Again you measure the discrepancy when you reach the target mark at the top tooth and make the necessary correction, whether larger or smaller. Work backward from the top towards the entrance until your marks again catch up to each other and coincide. Voila, you're done. This correction technique has proved very useful through the years.

If done correctly, you should only have to make one adjustment, reaching the top and then backtracking, although I have had some instances in which it took several attempts.

I have a practical saying when it comes to labyrinths: "If you want it to be right, don't do it wrong." By that I mean, keep at it, counting your lunation marks and adjusting your spacing until you have the right number, within a close tolerance. In so doing, you will assure that the lunations will come out right. Don't give up and accept error.

If using masking tape or stones on the ground, measure the diameter of the labyrinth and divide by thirty-six. This should be the spacing for the lunations, with just a little fudging required.

Making the lunation template

The somewhat complicated variables in making the lunations are handled quite well by the template design. This applies only to situations where the lunations are carefully constructed, such as on canvas or concrete. For painting on grass or using masking tape, in which the path/line units are not exact, simply divide the diameter of your completed labyrinth by 36. That will give you a very close approximation of the spacing. I usually mark a yardstick to use both for the spacing and the length of the teeth, to use as a guide. In such cases, I make the lunations as straight rays radiating outward, rather than making 112 little circles. Paradoxically, the lunations (moon cycles) make the labyrinth look like a big sun.

For precise lunations, you could, were you more fanatical than I, actually make two templates, one for the left side and another for the right side. This would be important if you were to design templates that were used as stencils, painting the lunations directly onto the surface. We did that when scoring the pattern into the concrete, as the tool was set to a certain lunation size.

Yet, in the hundreds of Chartres labyrinths that we have drawn on canvas and concrete, we have used one template and fudged in the manner that is described here.

There are three considerations in drawing the lunations.

1. The height of the teeth.
2. The width of the teeth.
3. The spacing of the circles.

Let's remind ourselves of the various proportions and relationships. For our example, we will use the actual full-size measurements for the Chartres labyrinth.

Once, in Chartres Cathedral, I wanted to measure the diameter of the lunation circle but I had no measuring device with me. I decided to just make marks on a piece of paper and measure them later. I pulled out a standard (in the United States) piece of 8½" x 11" letter-size paper. When I laid it across the lunation I said, "Oh, look at that!" The circle was the same diameter as the length of the paper, 11".

I then turned it the other way to measure the height of the tooth. It was just a little shorter than the width of the paper (about 8⅛") .

The path width that I use is 13¾" (taking into account some of the mortar) but in Chartres, the stone in the path itself is 13½". The line is 3". Hence the ratio of 4.5 : 1. For the following proportions I will use 13½", as that's what the mason of Chartres would have used.

Remember that a path/line unit is comprised of eleven units, two for the line and nine for the path. That's the 4.5 : 1 ratio. We do the same proportions for the lunations, starting with the path width. So if we divide 13 ½ by 11 we get 1.227. Two of those units equals the tooth width, ergo 2.455. Nine of the units, which equal 11.045, indicate the diameter of the lunation circle. This is also the height of the line/tooth unit. Since the line equals 3" the tooth must be 8.045".

With 11" as height of the tooth/line and width of the lunation circle, it gives a back and forth rhythm: space. . .tooth. . . space. . .tooth. . .horizontal. . .vertical. . .horizontal. . .vertical. The proportions are very pleasing to the eye.

I use 13¾" for the path width, 2½" for the tooth width, and 8⅛" for my tooth height (or slightly more). My line remains 3". Since I use one pattern for both sizes of lunations, I make it smaller, about 10¾".

Considering these measurements and proportions, let's take a look at the template and see how to make it and then put it to use.

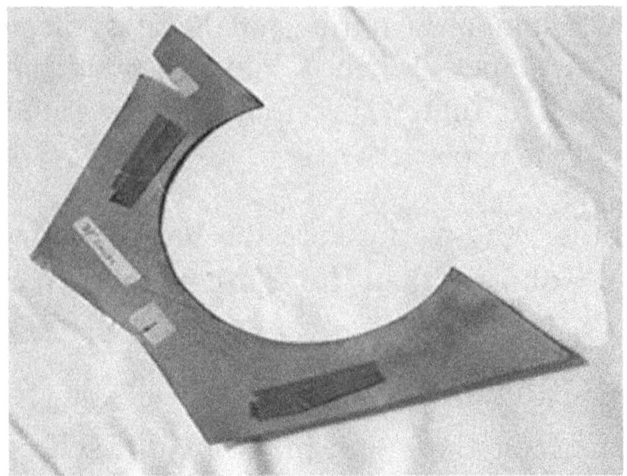

I draw the lunations in a clockwise direction. The notch in the left side of the template allows me to see the previously drawn lunation circle, so as to determine the proper width for the tooth.

Here's a diagram of the template (below).

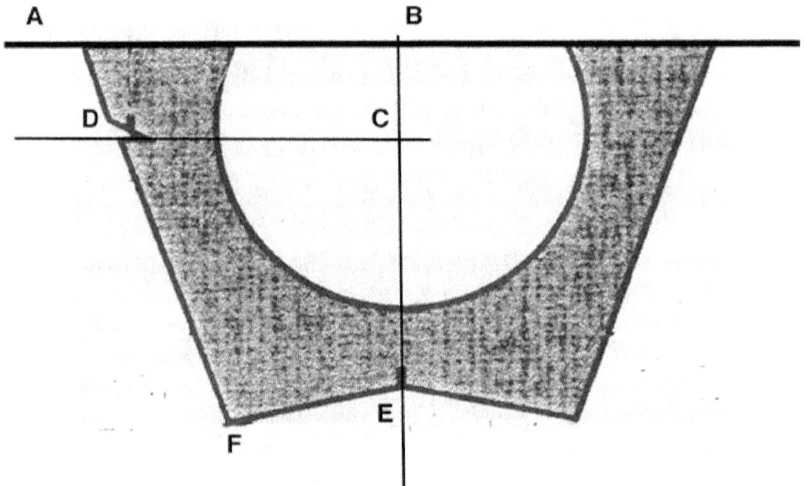

<u>A: Top of tooth</u>

The horizontal line labeled "A" represents the edge of the template material, be it cardboard or polycarbonate or sheet metal. The top of the template, along the line A, is where we will draw the tops of the teeth.

<u>B: First vertical</u>

The first step in making the template is to draw the vertical line that will serve as the central axis. If using poster board for a temporary pattern (for a single labyrinth), I usually use ballpoint pen or a fine marker. On plastic or metal, I use a Sharpie®.

I use a T-square to make the perpendicular line. If you don't have one, you can use your compass. Here's how. Make a mark on the edge of the template material where you want the vertical line to be (B in the illustration below). Set your compass to a convenient setting about half of its size capacity. For our example, let's say 3". Put the point of the compass on B and make two more marks (X), one on each side. Each will be 3" from the center mark.

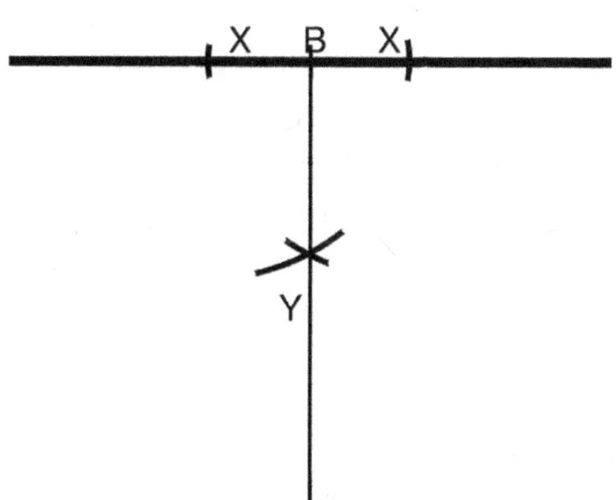

Now increase the span of the compass to, say, 6". Put the point of the compass on each X and make an arc below B. The two arcs will cross at Y, directly below B. Align a straightedge with B and Y and draw the vertical line.

<u>C: Center of circle</u>

In order to draw the lunation circle, we have to determine where the center is. Measuring down the vertical axis, the distance from point B to the lunation circle represents the height of the tooth. From the circle to point E represents the width of the twelfth circle (line).

We know the tooth to be 8⅛" tall. If the diameter of the lunation circle is 10¾", the radius would be 5⅜".

The distance from point B to point C indicates the difference between the tooth height and the lunation radius. In this case, that would be 8⅛" less 5⅜", which yields 2¾".

Measure 2¾" from point B down the vertical axis and make a mark. That will be the center of the lunation circle. Draw the circle using a compass. I use a clever compass that holds a ballpoint pen or marker.

D: Locating the tooth width notch

Off to the left somewhere measure down 2¾" (in this case) and draw a line from that point to C. This locates the notch for measuring the tooth width.

E: Determining line width

The distance from the bottom of the lunation circle to point E represents the width of the twelfth circle. Remember that we only drew 12-i, the inner circle, because the outer circle will be the lunations. The template is made to line up with 12-i. Therefore, it must allow for the width of the line before drawing the lunation circles. Hence point E. Make a mark here on your template, as it will be the point that you align with the spacing marks.

F: Template corners

There's no specific measurement for making the bottom edge of the template. I draw two perpendicular lines, one from each corner of the tooth (where the lunation circle meets the top of the pattern, line A). These lines are not shown. Then I make two marks, equidistant from and lower than point E (say 11½").

The template will be used on the twelfth circle. So the bottom of the template should take that into consideration. If it were flat on the bottom, the corners wouldn't reach the circle (12-i), making it hard to line up the template properly. The logic of my approach will become apparent shortly.

D. More about tooth width

The tooth width is about 2½" in our example. The notch in the side of the template can be any shape. I make a little "V" shape.

It could be a rectangular cutout, or a half circle. The important feature is for it to extend within 1¾" of the lunation circle.

Thus, when you make the tooth the proper width, the previous circle will be visible in that notch. I make a mark right on the template 2½" from the lunation circle. When we cover drawing the lunations, you will see how easy that makes our task..

Using the lunation template

First, let's practice using the template. Pick one side of the labyrinth and lay down long strips of masking tape sufficient to draw three of four lunations on the tape, rather than the surface. It will take five or six rows of masking tape, five or six feet long.

Evenly line up the template (the mark at E) with one of the lunation circle spacing marks on the twelfth circle (12-i). If the corners of the template overlap the twelfth circle (being a bit too long) that's no problem. Just put a mark on each corner where it hits 12-i. For the next lunation, line up the template with those marks on 12-i.

Draw (on the masking tape) one complete lunation circle by starting on the upper left, on the top flat part, ¼" to the left of the corner. Follow with your pencil around the corner, around the whole circle, and around the tip of the righthand corner, stopping on the flat surface ¼" to the right. What you drew should look like this:

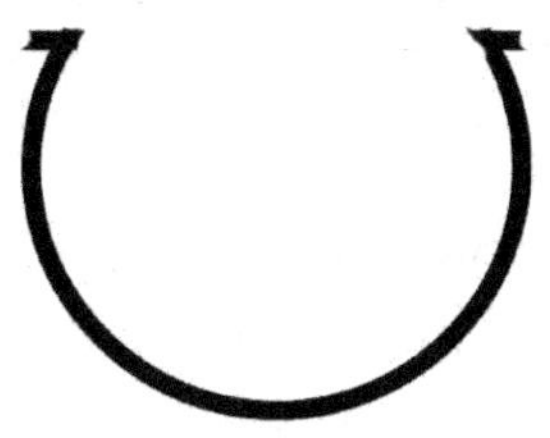

Later you can use a straightedge to go around and draw the tops of the teeth by connecting the little hooks that you have made.

Note: If you are painting the Chartres pattern on canvas, you will want to see our book *Canvas Labyrinths: Construction Manual.* It has many more tips. This manual is about understanding the pattern. That book is more about the physical act of drawing and painting. For example, if you draw a line to connect the lunation tips, painting those little corners is difficult and time consuming. Instead, put a piece of tape across the top of the tooth and paint right up onto the tape. When you remove the tape, you have excellent crisp corners. If you are using a tape machine, make an outer circle of tape to mark the tooth height. Then just draw (and paint) the circles up onto the tape without needing to hassle with those little corners.

After drawing that first lunation circle, we need to check the accuracy of the template. Measure the width of the twelfth circle from the lunation circle to 12-i. It should be your line width. If not, adjust the template by making new marks at the corners to raise or lower it.

Staying on the masking tape, let's draw a second lunation. On the template, make a mark by the notch indicating the proper width for the teeth (say, 2½"). This width will stay consistent, so that all the teeth look uniform. Any fudging will take place within the lunation circle, where it won't be noticed.

When preparing to make the next lunation circle, ignore the spacing mark. Instead, align the template in three places: the mark in the notch for the proper tooth width, and the two corners on circle 12-i. Once that's in place, look to see where the spacing mark is located compared to the center of the template (the mark at E). Since we are using one template, and since the lunations are different sizes on the right and left sides of the labyrinth, there will typically be a small space between the two marks.

This shows how much we need to fudge. Don't feel bad about fudging. It is what all craftsmen do to make sure their work comes out looking as good as possible. It's not cheating. Plus, it's downright necessary.

Below, the tooth width is properly aligned. At the bottom, the center of the pattern and the spacing mark don't quite line up. That's where fudging comes into play.

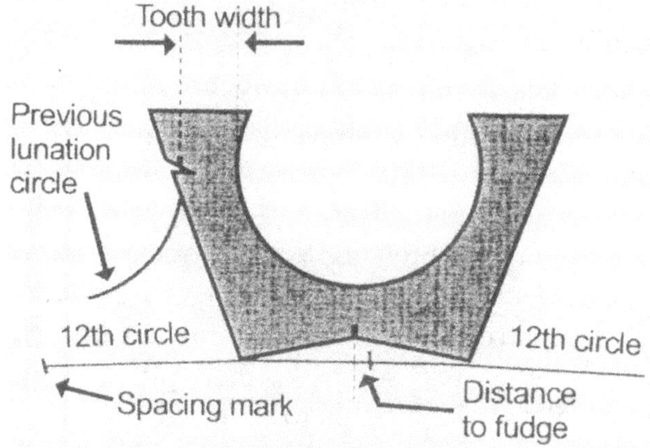

Start drawing with the template in the correct tooth width position, but only draw half the lunation circle. Stop at the bottom of the template. Then, move the template (in this case, to the right) so that the center mark matches up with the spacing mark.

Once the template is repositioned, draw the other half of the circle. Voila! That slight adjustment is not noticeable. With this easy technique, you can use the same template for all the lunations. This method also assures that any variation is spread out evenly over the whole labyrinth, rather than all accumulating at one place.

Draw three or four lunations on your masking tape area for practice. Now's the time to find any irregularities that need to be corrected. For example, if the lunation template is too small or too large, the gap may be too great to easily fudge. In dire situations I have fudged as much as half an inch, but that's not desirable. If the variation is too great, you should make a new template of a slightly different size.

Once you have practiced on the masking tape and made all necessary adjustments to the template, you are ready for the big time.

Starting at the entrance is difficult because the 12th circle stops causing half of the template to hang out into the entrance path. I suggest starting at the first mark and leaving the entrance until later, after gaining more skill and familiarity with the template.

Hold the template firmly so that it doesn't move. If the posterboard seems flimsy, tape something strong to the template, being careful that it doesn't jut out into the area in which you draw. (I use some six-inch plastic rulers that I bought in quantity, which helps to stiffen the template.) When using an aluminum template and drawing outside on concrete (using a Sharpie® felt-tipped pen), I sometimes use my knee to help hold the template in place. To draw on canvas, I use a mechanical pencil, as it doesn't require sharpening.

After drawing the first lunation circle, move the template, line up the tooth width and proceed as described above. Repeat one hundred and eleven more times.

Major fudging

Occasionally, I made a mistake in laying out the lunation spacing. All of a sudden I came to a gap of two or three inches between the two marks (template and spacing). This is too much to correct in one circle. However, it can be corrected over a group of circles. Suppose the error is 2", and you have at least sixteen lunations left to draw, you can fudge ⅛" on each lunation. Just as when correcting the spacing marks, you will see the error diminish with every lunation until you catch up to the correct spacing marks.

It is this ease in accommodating some fudging that can allow a gap of an inch or two (or even three) when marking out the lunation spacing (when arriving at the top target mark), as once you are drawing, you can fudge to get back to your proper spacing. You must be sure that you have enough lunations remaining to draw to accomplish the fudging.

If you are making a temporary labyrinth on the grass, none of the above precision is necessary. You won't need a template. Just follow the other general directions and everything will be fine.

You can make straight lines, like rays, for the teeth, or use several rocks or bricks to make a little triangle or even a partial circle for each lunation. Beware, if you use three bricks to make a lunation tooth, it will take 339 bricks to do them all.

With this last element, you have now completed drawing the Chartres pattern. That wasn't so bad, was it? There remain a few more hints.

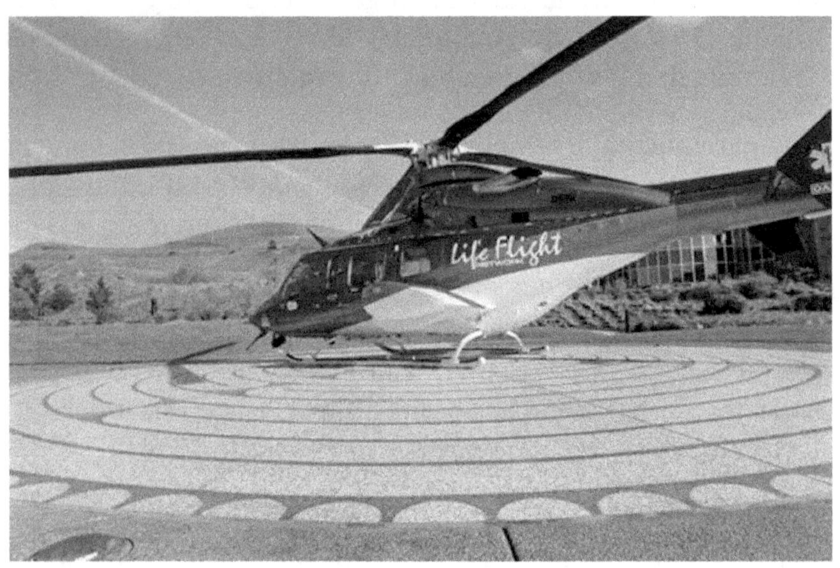

How many times making a labyrinth have people asked me if I'm constructing a helicopter pad. Well, here's an example at a hospital in Oregon that actually has a labyrinth on the helicopter pad. Photo courtesy of Jim Semlor Photographers.

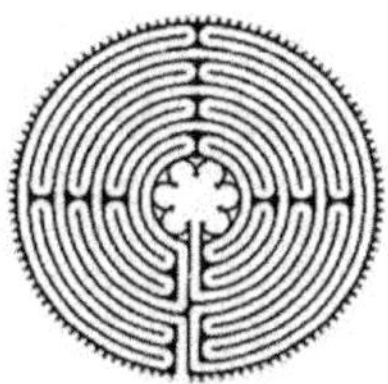

Pattern Variations

There are many variations to the Chartres labyrinth pattern. Technically, it's *not* correct to use the name Chartres just because it has some petals or lunations. For example, there are several five-circuit patterns that claim Chartres heritage. Bah humbug. I won't even include them here. They are atrocious.

Well, I must admit, we once offered such a pattern. Very stylized, we called it the Heart of Chartres (see below).

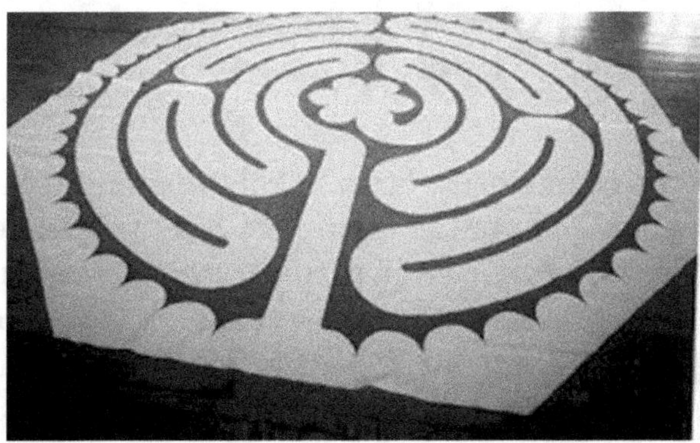

You can add lunations and petals to any pattern and then claim to be in the Chartres family. However, it is unlikely that it will have the appropriate sacred geometry, proportions, and design features to qualify for such a heritage.

One possible exception to my principled categorization would be certain 7-circuit patterns. My favorite is the Chartres Essence (below).

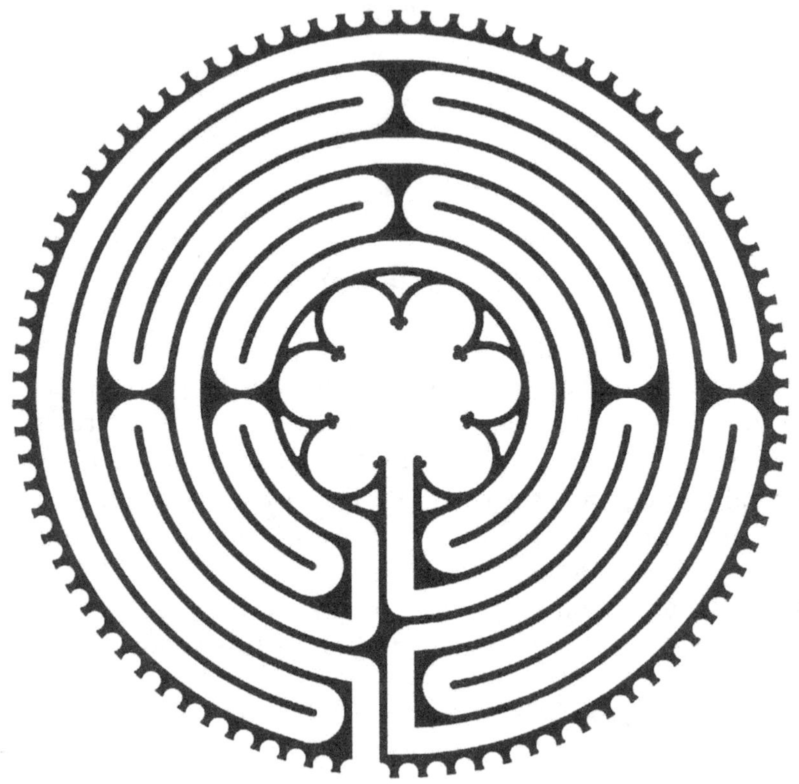

We make the center extra large in this version, to have more room for people to gather there. In fact, the center is the normal size for an 11-circuit pattern, even though this is 7-circuits. The full Chartres has four lunar months represented (112 lunation circles) whereas this has three months (84 lunation circles). I think the entrance most resembles the true Chartres appearance.

Neither this pattern nor any other that I have created are copyrighted or protected in any way. They are all in the public domain and available for any use. I believe copyright protection can be appropriate in some cases, but I don't claim it.

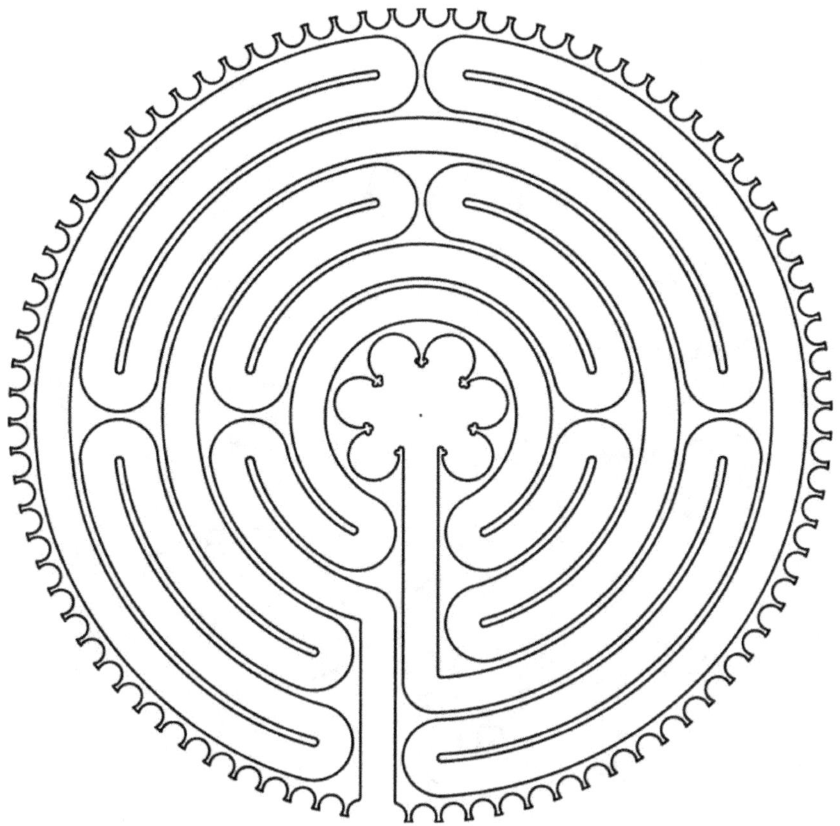

For many years we sold a pattern we called the Petite Chartres. I like the symmetry of the turns on the horizontal axis. The entrance is not very Chartres-like, however.

When reducing the Chartres pattern to seven circuits, a number of possibilities exist, depending on which seven circuits are chosen and which four are deleted. I have seen some in which the inner or outer seven circuits were used, which leads to an entrance path on an outer or inner circuit, which I especially dislike. It makes me think that you fall into (or out of) the labyrinth with little effort.

Another variation of the Chartres labyrinth involves changing the geometry in some way. In one case, we were asked to make a separate exit path for the Chartres.

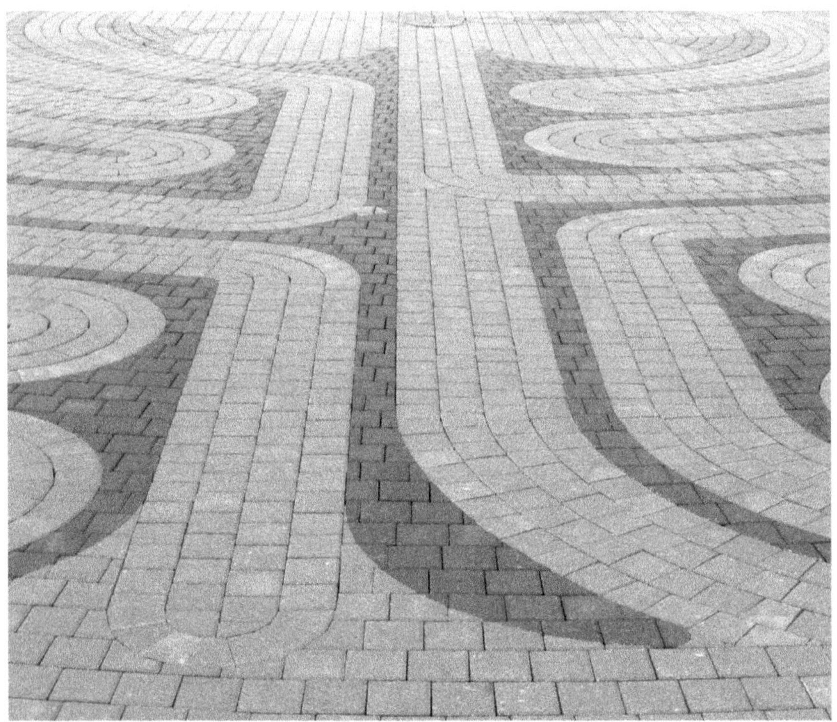

Here it is. This is at the University of Southern Indiana in Evansville, Indiana. There's actually an intersection, when coming to the last turn that leads into the center. To indicate the path, the pavers lead around to the right, into the center. Then, one can walk straight out.

Writing about the dedication of the labyrinth, a local journalist called me and asked, "Why do you need a separate exit path. Can't people just walk out at any time, from any place in the labyrinth?" Good point, for which I didn't have a good answer, except that's what the client wanted. The magnificent paver work (pavers are like bricks, but made of concrete) was done by my colleague Marty Kermeen (see his website at www.labyrinthsinstone.com). His work is so exact it looks like the pattern is painted on, but those are two colors of pavers, meticulously cut by hand and fitted together.

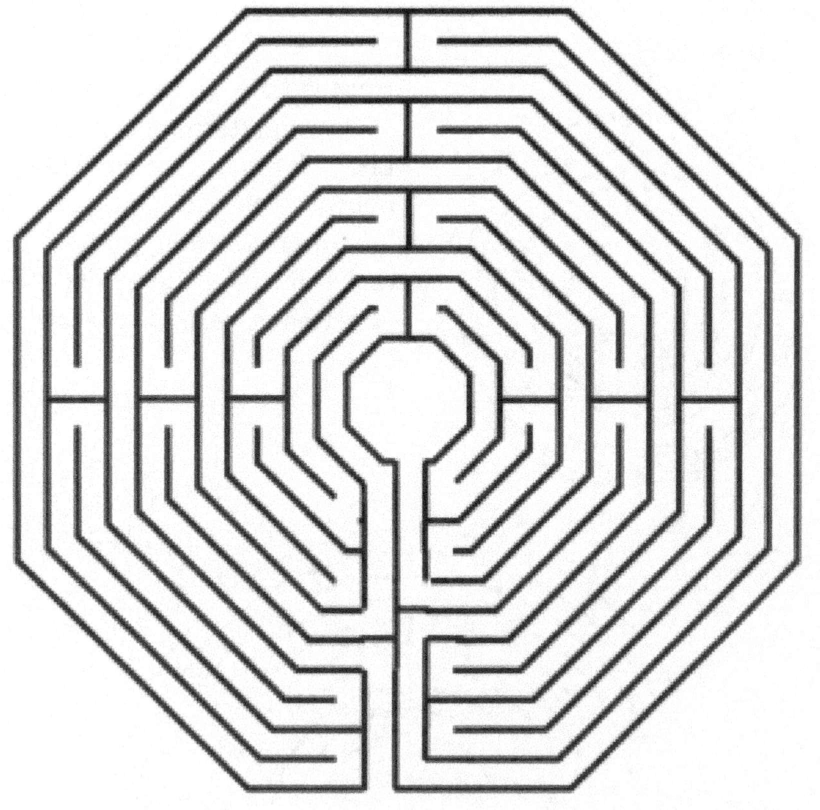

The path pattern for the Chartres labyrinth was developed in manuscript drawings over a period of several centuries, being finally realized some three hundred years before Chartres was built. However, it didn't have the petals, lunations or proportions that were prescribed in Chartres. In labyrinth circles (no pun intended) we call the pre-Chartres path pattern the medieval pattern. Only when you add the other details does it become the Chartres labyrinth.

Above is a medieval pattern made octagonal. If making the labyrinth out of square tiles, this would be a much easier than making circles, requiring only two angles to be cut (45 degrees and 22.5 degrees).

At my last labyrinth making master class, I made a new Chartres variation for the first time. We were talking about circular 7-circuit patterns that have the entrance paths aligned on the vertical axis.

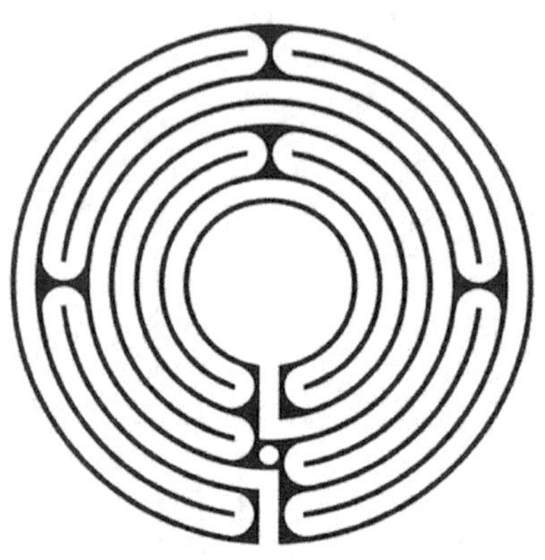

Here is an example, the Circle of Peace pattern, originated by Lisa Moriarty. I have known people to add petals and lunations to this pattern to make it look more like the Chartres pattern.

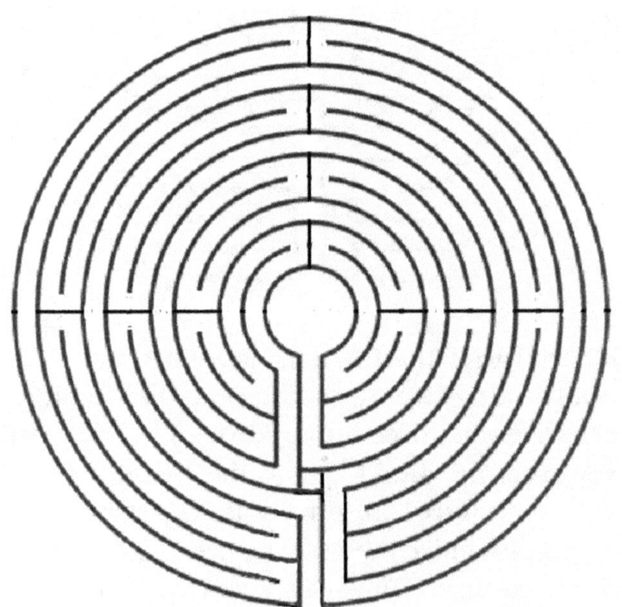

It occurred to me that we could align the entrance paths on the medieval or Chartres pattern. So I tried it (above). An aligned medieval pattern has potential. For one thing, the lunations would all be the same size, with an equal number on each side.

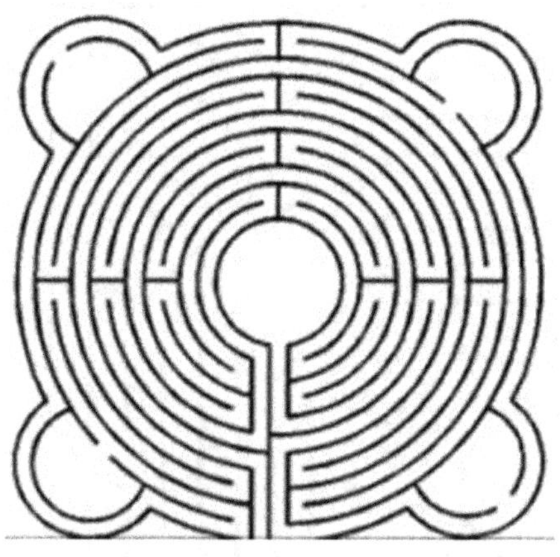

Another possibility is to add little bastions outside of the normal pattern. Here's an example. Notice that two bastions are entered from the outer eleventh path and two from the tenth path. You could put benches in these areas and give the walker a place to rest or meditate.

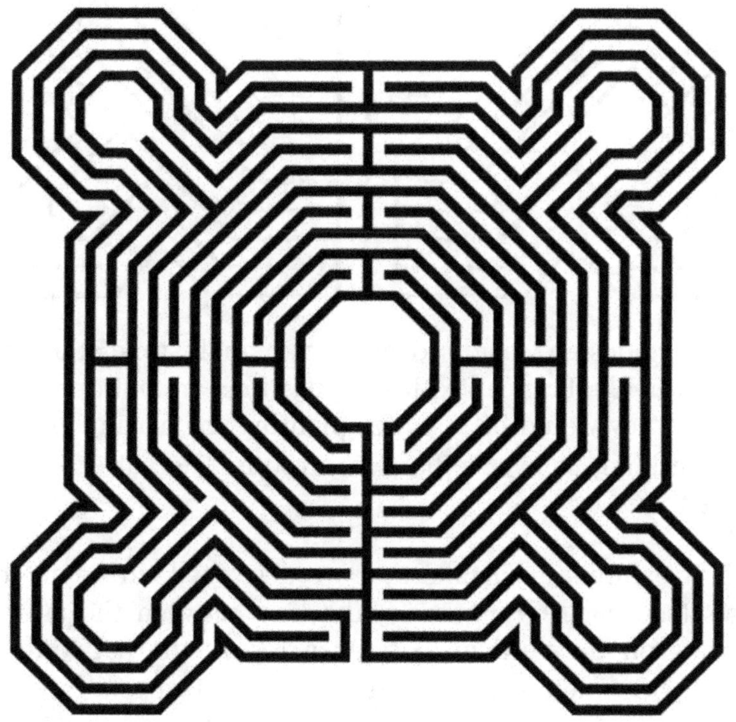

The labyrinth once found in Rheims, France, had significant bastions. This is also the symbol used in France for all historical monuments.

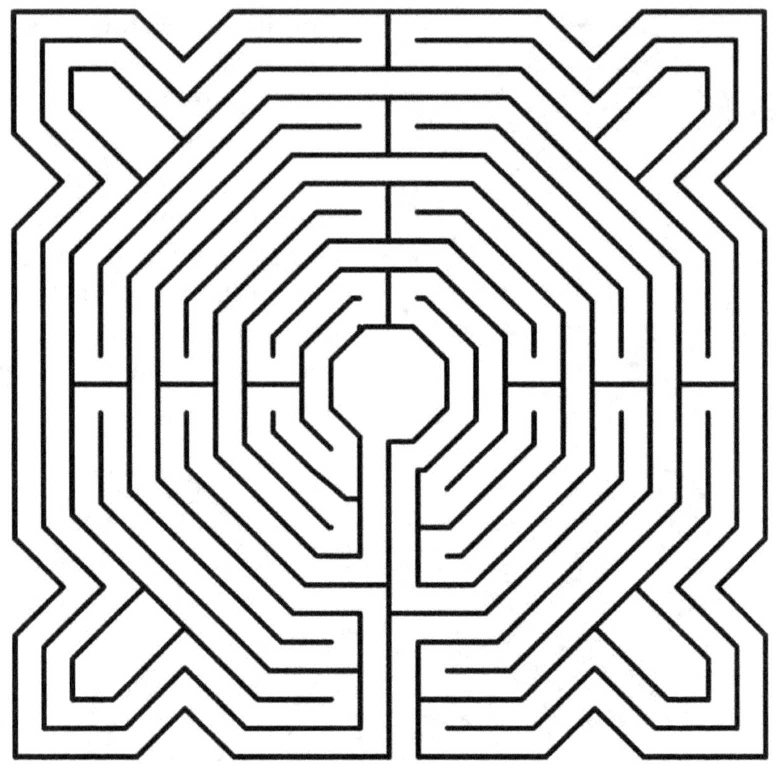

The above design was discovered on a small stone at a church in Genainville, France. Notice the bastions are not open to the walker. They would be good for plantings or placing an object of some kind, or even pillars in a room. The pattern is right handed.

Alas, it exhibits a mistake that we described earlier in these pages (see page 63), namely, the line between the entrance paths is on the vertical axis. As a result, the path into the center becomes offset to one side. Bastions give the appearance of corners making a circular pattern look square.

I once designed a contemporary labyrinth that had internal bastions, with benches in them to give the walkers a place to sit and meditate or rest.

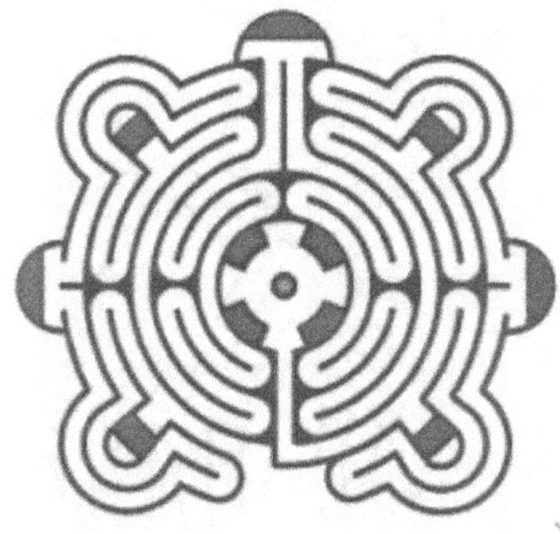

A contemporary pattern with seven bastions containing benches. In the center are four more benches.

When entering the Chartres labyrinth, you encounter a line across the entrance that turns the path to the left and then back again to the entrance. I have called this the detour. The same "blocking" principle makes a bastion. The more paths that are blocked, the more that go around the bastion.

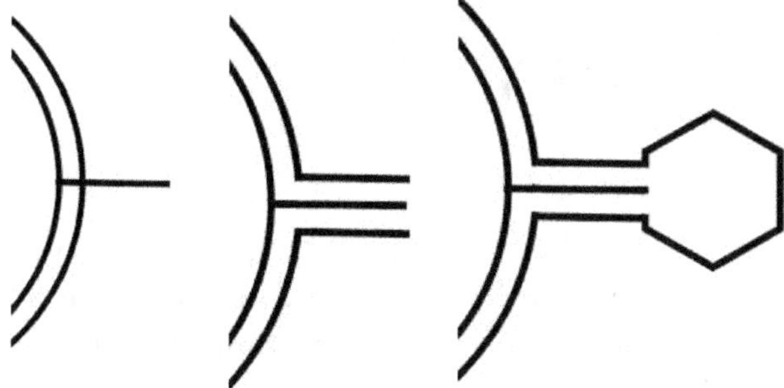

Making bastions involves a three-step process. 1. Block one or more paths with a line. 2. Turn the path. 3. Add the bastion (whatever shape desired). I think this has much design potential, adding interest, more turns, and a practical purpose to the pattern.

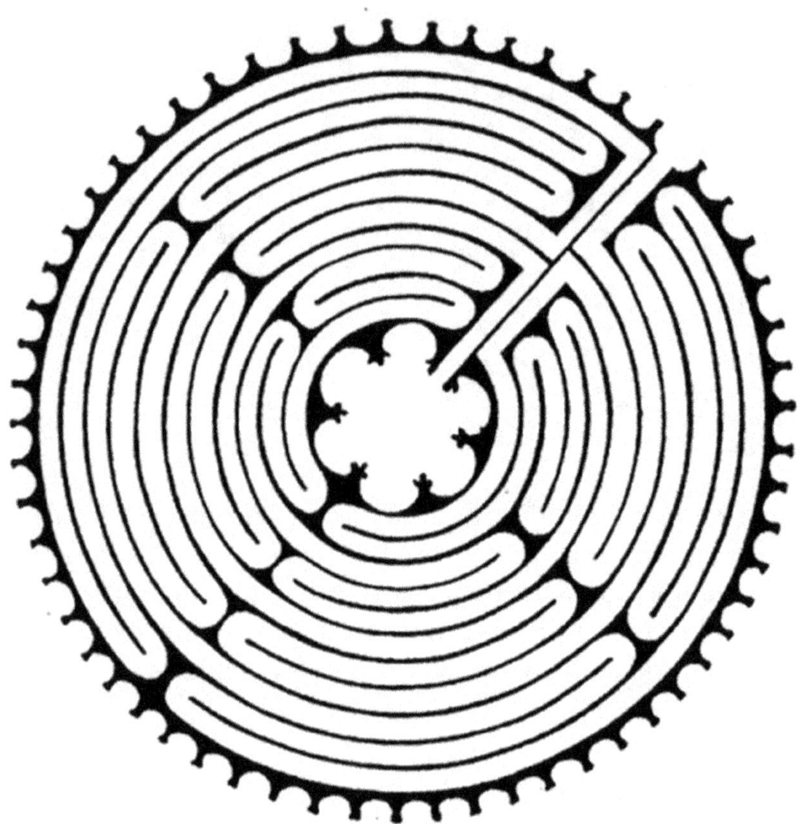

The above drawing of the Chartres labyrinth used to bug me because the lunations are so huge and out of proportion. There are only fifty-eight of them. Fifty-six would be two lunar months, but I'm sure they had no understanding of the lunations or their symbolism.

However, with very small labyrinth drawings, the lunations become hard to see. So, I have relaxed my criticism if the intent in drawing huge lunations is for graphic clarity. But it's still ugly.

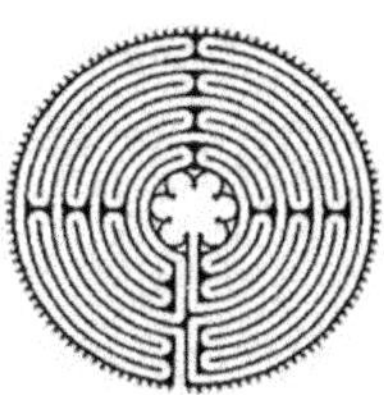

Other Considerations

Using volunteers

Constructing your own labyrinth builds community and rapport. When we install a labyrinth using our crushed granite technology, Linda and I go by ourselves and direct local workers and volunteers in what to do. Besides reducing the cost, this allows churches and other clients to be involved in the construction of their labyrinth.

Linda and I drew and painted a Santa Rosa pattern on a 24-foot canvas. No longer having a studio, we used the dance floor in the clubhouse of our over fifty-five community. Several friends came and helped get the work done, as we had the space for only two days.

Similarly, I recently directed volunteers to draw and paint a custom designed canvas labyrinth at Church of the Holy Spirit in San Antonio. Some of the volunteers were so good that I would gladly hire them to be crew members, except that I am retired now (sort of).

In my experience, the volunteer with the least talent usually rushes right to the most important places (center, petals, entrance) to begin working. That's why I have volunteers paint on sample material (or cardboard) to determine if they can keep within the lines. Many can, but some don't even come close.

If someone can't paint precisely, I don't hesitate to assign them other duties (fixing lunch, cleaning brushes . . .). Alternatively, I have had people lay down masking tape on both sides of the lines. This is time consuming, but if done right can give good results for the less than steady-handed. Once the labyrinth is taped, the painting goes quickly. It requires special tape.

I gave a workshop in Perth, Australia, which included making a canvas labyrinth. People paid to come and learn that skill, which in turn paid for the sponsor to hire me. So she got a free labyrinth. We worked outdoors on a paved area (with a tarp under the canvas), to the sound of kookaburras and Linda's flute music.

Unfortunately, most of the class failed the painting skill test and there was no time to tape the pattern. I ended up staying an extra day in order to finish the painting.

Although I am likely the most experienced and skilled worker, most of my time is spent supervising and teaching others, with the result being that volunteers make most of the labyrinth. It may be a bit more rustic, but that's okay. The love and joy that goes into it makes the project worthwhile.

There's an upper limit on the number of possible volunteers. I would say five or six is the maximum on the labyrinth, with others providing support. In labor intensive situations (pavers, crushed stone), many more can be utilized.

I frequently tell clients that I could do the project myself in around seven days, or, with volunteers, in nine days. Even though volunteers make the work more time consuming, I charge less for the project.

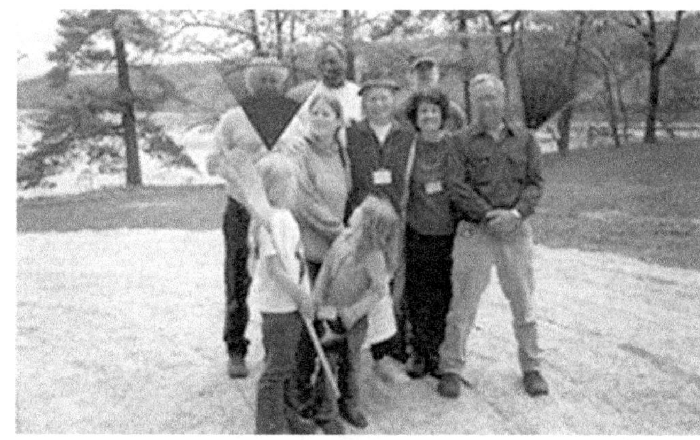

Volunteers (left) who constructed the brick-and-mulch labyrinth (below) at Silver Bay, New York, a YMCA retreat center on Lake George.

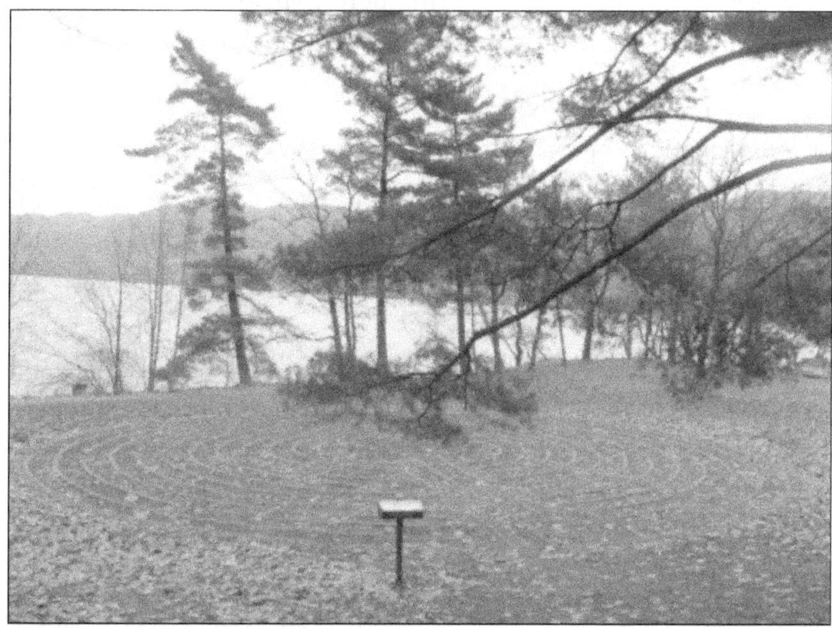

Even when we have a full crew of our own workers, sometimes volunteers bring water and snacks and meals (and in one instance, bread pudding, having learned it's my favorite). Some churches signed up volunteers to invite us to supper each evening (for which First Presbyterian Church in Livermore, California, set a standard unlikely ever to be surpassed).

When working with young volunteers, attention span becomes an issue. It's hard for them to work more than ten minutes without taking pictures of themselves and texting friends.

At one middle school, I thought the young people were aloof, disinterested, and working against their will. Only later did I learn that they went home and bragged to their parents about the great labyrinth they helped to construct. Go figure.

When we work with volunteers, we create a meditative space with soft music, asking for a minimum amount of conversation. Not only does this help concentration, it makes the whole activity a spiritual process rather than a gossip fest.

We start painting in more obscure areas so the workers can get some practice before attacking the more difficult tasks. Painting outdoors on concrete with volunteers, I once had the steady-handed workers use their brushes the narrow way to paint carefully along the outer edges. Then, the less steady people came along behind and filled in the center portion.

In some cases, volunteers are not worth what they are paid (zero). I have had jobs where none of the scheduled volunteers bothered to even show up. Others seem to have trouble following instructions. But in the end, it's usually a pleasant experience, eventually standing in awe of the labyrinth we made together.

Ceremony

Make a ritual out of every step of painting and using your labyrinth. Bless the unpacking of the canvas or the marking out of the concrete, bless your paint and brushes and tools, bless your hands that they may be steady. When the work is done, plan to celebrate and give recognition due.

I have always wanted to have the time and resources to give the workers T-shirts or other momentos, and certificates saying they helped to install the labyrinth. A brochure about the labyrinth can include the names of those who helped build it.

Make a special event of the first person who walks the labyrinth. (The donor would be a good candidate.)

One of the greatest benefits of making labyrinths is the satisfaction that so many people will use them for their well-being.

Do not, I say again, do not schedule the dedication of the labyrinth until it's finished. I know of numerous occasions where big events were scheduled and advertised only to find that an unexpected circumstance delayed the completion of the labyrinth. I even put in my installation agreement that I am not responsible if the labyrinth isn't finished by the dedication date.

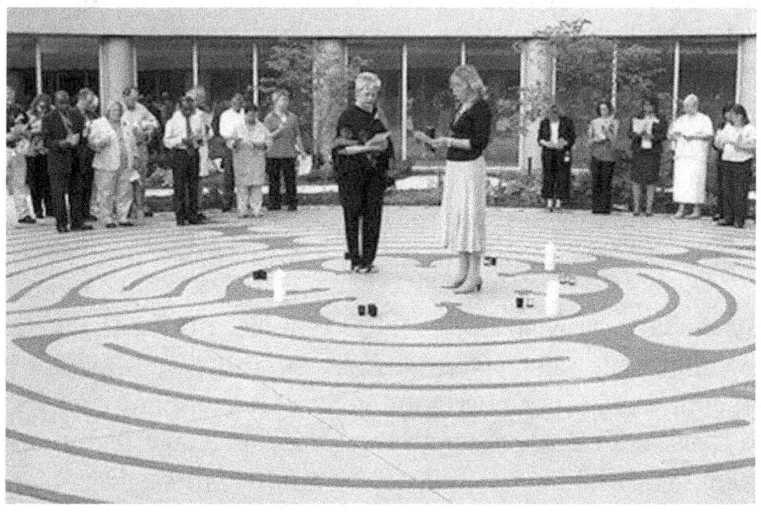

Dedication of labyrinth at Marianjoy Rehabilitation Hospital, Wheaton, Illinois. Photo courtesy of Marianjoy Rehabilitation Hospital.

What kind of dedication should you have? Warren Lynn has a plethora of useful information on his website, the Well Fed Spirit (see www.wellfedspirit.org). I went to one dedication of a labyrinth in which the bishop never once mentioned the labyrinth. That was a bit strange.

One dedication used the scripture story of the Road to Emmaus, in which the resurrected Jesus walked with the disciples but they didn't recognize him. On a labyrinth, you never know who may be walking with you.

Building with other materials

Labyrinths have been built from an amazing variety of materials. The only requirement is to designate the path. For example, you can put things on the ground, such as sticks, rocks, bricks, bottles, driftwood, or cans of food. I have used wooden blocks on a parking lot. Or you can stick things into the ground, such as surveyor's flags, plastic spoons, or turkey feathers (all of which have been done).

I know of beautiful labyrinths made of granite, inlaid parquet wood, hand-shaped brick pavers, and mosaic work. The possibilities are endless.

The continental divide of labyrinth building is the distinction between soft surface and hard surface materials. Soft surface includes paths of grass, sand, or mulch. They can be made quite inexpensively and are usually do-it-yourself projects.

Hard-surface labyrinths usually require professional help, using materials such as stone, pavers and concrete. For the cost, concrete gives a very good value. My company, Labyrinth Enterprises, LLC, developed several proprietary technologies for making durable, low maintenance labyrinths using polymer concrete and crushed granite overlay. These are vastly superior to painting and staining. (For examples, photos and descriptions see www.labyrinth-enterprises.com/ourwork.html.

Join the labyrinth community

Here are three opportunities for anyone with a labyrinth, or an interest in them.

Veriditas

Founded in 1995 by the Rev. Dr. Lauren Artress at Grace Cathedral, Veridias remains the most active organization to promote labyrinths and train people in how to use them. I got my beginning as a labyrinth maker providing canvas labyrinths to Veriditas. You have surely noticed that the proceeds from this special Veriditas Edition go to that organization. Annually, in July or August, I give a master class in how to make labyrinths, sponsored by Veriditas. For a schedule of events see www.veriditas.org.

The Labyrinth Society

Founded in 1998, TLS has this mission statement:

> *"To support all those who create, maintain and use labyrinths, and to serve the global community by providing education, networking and opportunities to experience transformation."*

An annual gathering is held each year in the fall which is very rewarding to attend. The website is very informative. If you love labyrinths you should be a member of TLS. See www.labyrinthsociety.org.

The World-Wide Labyrinth Locator

Wouldn't it be nice when traveling to have a way to find any labyrinths in the area? The Labyrinth Locator, co-sponsored by Veriditas and The Labyrinth Society, lists thousands of labyrinths all over the world. If you make a labyrinth and want the public to know about it, be sure to upload information to this site (a form is provided). See: www.labyrinthlocator.com.

Well Fed Spirit
A number of photos in this and my other labyrinth books have come from Warren Lynn. As Executive Minister of Christian Vocations for The Christian Church (Disciples of Christ) he has assembled a website with an astounding amount of labyrinth information. You could read it for weeks. See:
http://wellfedspirit.org/spirituality_pages/labyrinths.html

This is just the beginning

Although this book is coming to an end, your work in building labyrinths has an unlimited future. Because this book is produced by a very friendly and accessible technology, we plan to update it regularly. In that regard please send any corrections, comments, suggestions, photos, or other input to me:

robert@labyrinth-enterprises.com

My biggest concern is that what I am trying to explain, the details for making a labyrinth, is so clear to me that I think the reader will easily understand. But that may not be the case. If there was something unclear, if I went too fast, if I left something out, please take the time to let me know. As I am dyslexic, I may have transposed letters or numbers. Working together we can make this the best possible instruction manual.

Reviews are the lifeblood of self-publishing. If you liked this book, please go to Amazon or wherever you bought it and leave a favorable review. If you didn't like it, don't bother. Thanks for your time and energy in reading this book.

Resources

If you would like some help in constructing a labyrinth, besides myself, here are the folks I recommend.

Lisa Moriarty

I am putting Lisa first because she has made the commitment to be a full-time labyrinth maker. A former president of The Labyrinth Society, she makes labyrinths in all media, portable and permanent. She originated the labyrinth design called the Circle of Peace.
www.pathsofpeace.com

Lars Howlett

Lars is a professional photographer and labyrinth maker who apprenticed under me. He will be taking labyrinths to new heights in the future after us old fogies are gone.
www.discoverlabyrinths.com

John Ridder

John is a long time colleague who has been making labyrinths as long as I have. He also sells finger labyrinths and other products.
www.paxworks.com

Lea Goode-Harris

Lea originated the Santa Rosa labyrinth, of which we have made more than one hundred thirty. She has designed some wonderful custom labyrinths.
www.labyrinthtales.com

Marty Kermeen

Marty is hands down the world's greatest paver and stone labyrinth maker. If the budget doesn't fit pavers, he also can do crushed granite overlay.
www.labyrinthsinstone.com

Chuck Hunner
Chuck has served for more than a decade as my number one onsite supervisor. An especially talented jeweler (I wear one of his silver Chartres belt buckles every day), he is excellent with tools and precision (even more obsessed than I am). He has been generous in his appreciation of learning labyrinth construction, which he now does independently.
www.goldenspirit.com

Jeff Saward
Jeff is the world's greatest authority on labyrinths. Although he's in England, he's available for commissions. He also has the worlds largest collection of labyrinth photographs. His website is a trove of information.
www.labyrinthos.net

There's a whole new generation of people who make labyrinths. If you go to the Labyrinth Society, they have a list. I have conspicuously left out David Tolzmann and the Labyrinth Company. He doesn't choose to be part of the labyrinth community. Maybe it's sour grapes on my part, as he's the only one who has made any serious money selling labyrinths (or kits and templates). He has a huge presence on the internet. You're not very likely to miss seeing him. Or to like him.

I haven't included a list of internet resources as I have already mentioned the organizations and people that I favor. One of my favorite pastimes, however, is to search for labyrinths under Google Images. All kinds of interesting and unusual things come up. Also a lot of mistaken history and weird ideas. Hey, it's the internet.

I have also left off a bibliography. There are several good ones on the internet including at my website and the Labyrinth Society. I don't know of any other book on labyrinth construction that I would recommend.

Thanks for reading. I hope to hear from you.

Robert Ferré

San Antonio, Texas
December, 2014
robert@labyrinth-enterprises.com
www.labyrinth-enterprises.com

www.ingramcontent.com/pod-product-compliance
Lightning Source LLC
LaVergne TN
LVHW010103110826
845155LV00028B/462

* 9 7 8 1 9 4 0 8 7 5 9 0 3 *